Gardening
with Kids

by Christine Rosakranse, PhD

Level
101

A fun guide to
growing healthier
together through
organic gardening

Extra
Credit

With special,
stress-less projects
you and your littles
can do together!

> **The best time to plant a tree was 20 years ago. The second best time is now.**
>
> **Chinese Proverb**

So you want to garden with kids!?

Have you always wanted to garden ... anc you have one or more children? This means that you have plenty of free time and energy for an arduous, time-consuming enterprise wrought with unnecessary stress, right? Wrong. This is not what I want for you or your family.

This book is aimed at families that want to learn about gardening, grow healthy food, and create a family bond in nature. And it will provide you with some practical information so that this goal will be relatively stress-free.

We will also be promoting organic growing supported by permaculture methodologies. If these words are new to you or your kids, don't worry. Everything will be explained with full steps, supplies, and extra credit learning opportunities.

So I'll ask you again. Are you ready to garden...with kids?! Let's do it! And let's make it fun for both the grown-ups AND the kids! This is best done by first explaining the process in detail, allowing for changes to suit you and your family. That way you can have fun while letting your kids be kids.

Growing melons is one of the most interesting and rewarding projects that you can undertake with your children. Save seeds from the tastiest melon that you eat and save it for next year's growing season.

Photo: Indoor manual pollination. Bee suit optional

Raised beds are a great option for growing in difficult soil conditions

>> Page 54

Gardening with kids should be mostly fun and entirely educational. Feel free to move around the book to review different parts of starting a garden as suits your current season. Reading this book in the fall, start and the beginning and work your way through. Starting this book after you've already planted, skip ahead to the maintenance section and try implementing organic options for taking care of your family garden.

>> Page 30

Nasturtiums are a sure-fire way to add color and fun vines to your growing area. The plus side is that they can help with pest control and the flowers are edible, peppery and sweet at the same time.

>> Page 42

Table of Contents

Trays with 6 cells are the perfect size for starting seeds for a smaller home garden.

01

Before you jump ahead... Your first real step: Goals.

>> Step one is getting some seeds and throwing them in some dirt, right? Nope. The first step is to figure out what your goals are. Feel free to brainstorm with your children and get them started with you in the process. Your goals, wishes, and aspirations can be concrete or abstract. I've included a list on the next page that you can borrow from and add to.

Goals can be anything from fun to practical. They can be basic or fantastical. Just keep you and your family in mind. You know who you are and what you can handle. The same goes for your kids.

Goals

Below is a beginners list of goals. Once again, you know you and your family. What learning style best suits your kids or what subjects are they really into in school or homeschool? Do you need to find something that will hold their attention better than an electronic device? How does one spark intrinsic motivation (doing something because it makes you feel inherent satisfaction) versus extrinsic motivation (doing something for a reward)?

Growing healthy food

Growing healthy food that your kids will eat

Family bonding .

Getting out in nature

Saving the bees

Learning organic practices that will not poison you, your family, or the earth

Getting more Vitamin D into your system

Learning about vitamins and minerals in vegetables

Growing your own medicine

Becoming enchanted by the wonders of flowers

Feeding your need for creativity

Unleashing your inner scientist

Developing confidence

Unleashing your inner artist

Unleashing your inner foodie

Grounding

Growing (as a person, too!)

I just want to do a fun, rewarding thing - Growing a vegetable and then eating that vegetable is very rewarding!

Supplement classroom education

Supplement a homeschool science/home ec/art/math curriculum

Have fun!

Laugh!

Be a kid!

Be a kid again!

Additional goals:

_____

_____

_____

The freshest, most nutritious vegetables and herbs will always come from your home garden.

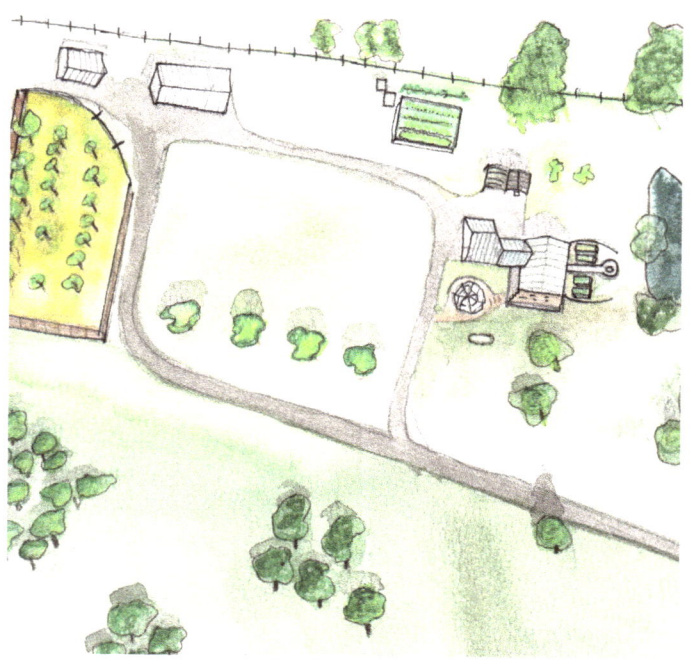

Your goals set the rules for your garden planning approach.

>> Don't forget about aesthetics! It's not silly for one of your goals to be making your home beautiful.

Goals can include growing varieties that you can't get at the local store, like this crimson amaranth or organic nasturtium with edible, but fragile flowers.

We have our goals. Now what?

Now that you have your goals, you can use them as a reference point for the projects you want to take on. For example, let's say you have a picky eater that repeatedly rejects any vegetable that you offer up on the dining room table. Your goals would include growing a garden that your child will eat, but you also have the additional goal of getting them to even try vegetables or fruits.

Having your son or daughter actually place the seed in the soil, tamp it down, water it, and watch it grow will turn that "icky" vegetable into an accomplishment in and of itself. Furthermore, you can turn that initial hesitancy into a science experiment which turns "ick" in interest. There are a few ways to do this.

TURN "ICK" INTO AWESOME

Because you can buy a greater variety of fruit and vegetable seeds or starts than the fruits and vegetables offered at the local grocery store, you can look for unique varieties that are sweeter, more colorful or even more alien-looking - anything - to get your kid to just try it. I will make more suggestions later in the book, but cherry tomatoes are a great example of a "gateway" vegetable.

Sungold and Sunrise Bumblebee are two varieties of cherry tomato that are brighter and sweeter than a normal tomato. Just imagine your little one walking up to a plant that they grew, plucking a ripe tomato and saying "Wow, mommy! Look what I grew. It is so delicious."

Another way to make veggie tasting "cool" is to grow some varieties that look like one thing, but taste like another. Golden berries, aka Physalis Peruvianus, are technically in the nightshade family (like tomatoes and peppers), but they are a delicious fruit with a vibrant, slightly pineapple-y flavor. They are fruity sweet tomatoes that come in a little husk packaging. They make the perfect snack and you have to unwrap them, which makes them like little "presents".

Purslane is a common weed with small succulent leaves that taste like citrus. You might already have it somewhere on your property. Before you eat it make sure that it isn't by the side of the road and that it hasn't been sprayed with weed killer.

Both purslane and golden berries are unique plants that are high in antioxidants and other minerals. Mint is also neat to eat all on its own, but there are a myriad of varieties that taste like lemon or chocolate that are sure to win over any non-herbivore. I'm pretty sure not liking vegetables does not pertain to chocolate mint leaves. Of course, you never know until you try.

Just imagine your little one walking up to a plant that they grew, plucking a ripe tomato and saying,

"Wow, mommy! Look what I grew. It is so delicious."

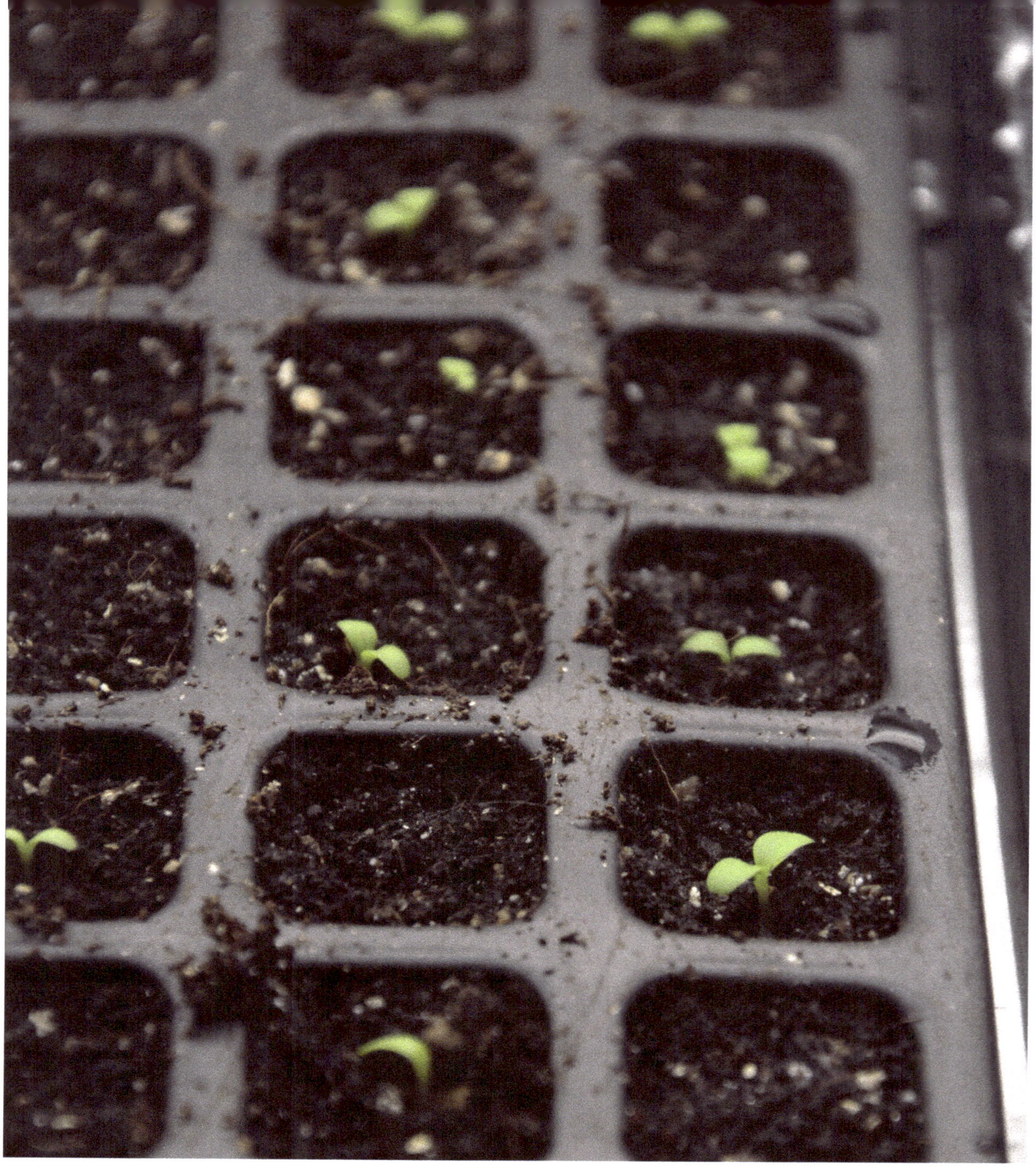

PROCESSING CENTER
STORAGE CONTAINER

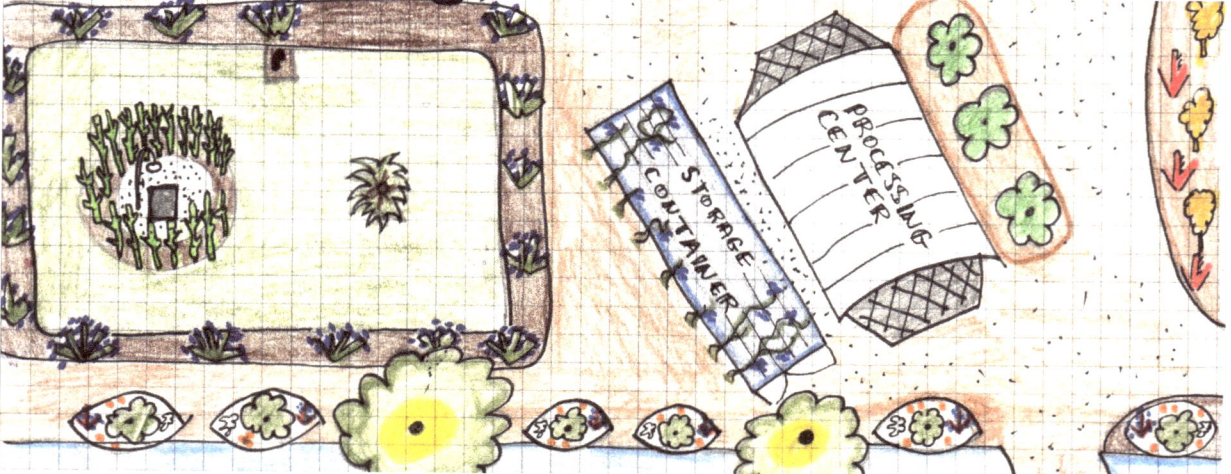

MATCHING GOALS TO YOUR RESOURCES

Let's be honest. Your access to resources is both a restriction and an opportunity. After all, we have to work with what we have. So first we must take stock. How much space do we have to grow? Do we need to use pots, raised beds, or are we sowing directly into the ground? It could be a combination. What is our budget? This is a two-pronged question. Ideally, anything that we grow in terms of food offsets future grocery expenditures. Grow now to save later. If you think of growing a garden as part of your child's learning experience, then you can count seeds, dirt, and pots as teaching supplies. [Can a tax person tell me if this is a write-off?]

Maximizing growing space is the most cost effective option that we have. Of course, there is a certain amount of land that one would need to grow enough food to feed a family of 4, for example. High density growing in a warm climate on 1.76 acres could feed a vegetarian family of 4 for the entire year. When you add in meat and dairy, this estimate rises to around 2 acres.

If we have less than that amount of space, then we would look at supplementing our food intake and reducing the cost of groceries. What does this mean for different sizes of property? If we have just a balcony, then we want to think in terms of spices, treats, or other high-value crops that will maximize the output from a smaller space input. Balconies and smaller spaces are also an opportunity for multi-level growing options.

Can you hang pots from the ceiling? Are you south-facing and can therefore do a "living wall" of herbs or succulents? Keep your plants small, harvest often, and you can grow a lot of them in this smaller space. Dwarf citrus fruits are also an option. Get creative, think vertical, and feel free to move stuff around to get the best results. But also be practical. In other words, you will not grow a watermelon unless you only want to grow a watermelon and little else.

In addition to space and money, time is both a resource and restriction. Indeed, time is the ultimate tradeoff. We can go to the grocery store now and buy tomatoes for $2 a pound or we can grow tomatoes from seed for 10 cents a pound (including the price of seeds, water, and soil), but we invest two months or more of passive time.

Other resources include access to free mulch, planters and pots, soil, or seeds. Some cities provide free wood chips as do some arborist companies. Most of the time, they have to pay to take this to the dump, so you can get it for free, if you have the room. Planters and pots can also be free, especially if you join a gardening group on your social media site of choice. Long time gardeners who buy lots of starts tend to have an abundance of the black nursery pots of various sizes.

Sometimes you can get free compost or manure if you live near farmland. Just be careful that it hasn't been sprayed or that the feed provided to the animals, be it hay or fresh grass, has not been sprayed with weed killers. These chemicals can actually survive the gastrointestinal tract and turn that free manure into plant killer soil.

If you do get a batch like this that kills your seedlings, you have two options: scrape it off and start over or look up remediation techniques online. Some of these remediation techniques include using mycorrhizae, a fungus, to help digest the dangerous chemicals or growing plants that specifically draw toxic chemicals from the soil. You also have to make sure that you age manure to ensure that any pathogens in the manure die from heat over time. This includes chicken, cow, and horse manure.

Necessity is the mother of invention

Proverb

Gardening on a balcony, patio, or other small space creates both a limitation and gives you the ability to get creative.

Think vertical!

Multi-level growing using metal shelves, hanging coco coir pots, repurposing a ladder, or using a trellis are all options for a modern family garden.

Goal Attainment: Growing Long-term Storage Crops

When we talk about goals helping you to determine your plan, here is an example. One of your goals may be to grow food that you can store and eat over the winter. This goal also pertains to trying to eat more locally grown food and seasonal produce.

Then your plan will include growing shelf-stable crops, like garlic, onions, potatoes, pumpkins, and other winter squashes. Other foods can be grown and stored after processing, but these are the main staples that can be stored anywhere that is cool and dry. No special steps are needed (except for curing for the alliums).

Eating according to the season is how humans have developed over the course of millenia. Pumpkins, potatoes, carrots, and onions are some crops that you will have available all winter into next year and these also happen to be the foods that are the most nourishing during a cold, hard winter. These are comforting, nourishing foods that will help you and your family to feel full and satisfied when it is cold outside.

Once we have a goal and the crops in mind that fulfill this, we can then plan for growing these crops. For a family of four, how many onions do you want to grow to be able to store some of them over the winter? How many kabocha squash? How many pounds of carrots?

This will depend on what you like to cook and what your family likes to eat. Some of us cook with garlic every meal. Some of us have never even heard of a kabocha squash.

Because we are starting at Garden Basics: 101 we are not shooting for 100% self-sufficiency. But there is great satisfaction and joy in knowing that whatever extra you have of these long-term food storage crops can be stored for later use. You and your kids grew food to eat and some extra to store. Next year you can do more. The first step of starting is the most important. You can always evolve and grow over time.

More preservation options are offered at the end of the harvest section (pg. 89).

Garlic comes in a number of varieties. Try ones that you can't get in your local grocery store.

Carrots can be stored throughout the winter

Garlic is a great crop to grow and can be saved or used for

Potatoes store well as long as they are kept cool and shady

Organic growing with the use of chemical pesticides and herbicides means that your children can roam through nature without worrying about getting poisoned.

On Organic Permaculture Methods

So let's get to the nitty griity. All suggestions in this book for your garden plan are based on an organic, permaculture design perspective. So let's review these terms.

ORGANIC

What does organic really mean anyway and why is it so important? Organic gardening means that we are not using poisonous chemical pesticides and herbicides to kill pests and weeds. The problem with chemicals designed to kill bugs and weeds is that they will also kill other things. One serious example being your body's own gut biome. And it will also have very detrimental effects on surrounding vegetation. Glyphosate, the main

A healthy garden supports a healthy family. Permaculture supports a healthy earth as well.

Permaculture means growing with nature, instead of going against it.

ingredient in RoundUp, has been shown to increase the risk of Non-Hodgkin lymphoma by 41%. Other digestion related diseases, such as Irritable Bowel Syndrome, leaky gut, and food allergies stem from

damage to the gut biome caused by non-organic food and other factors, including pesticides and PFAS, or forever chemicals that do not degrade over time. You have to use these products according to the instructions to ensure a "safe" outcome. Putting a child or any human in contact with even a small amount of these poisons is not safe. To be honest, I don't even like walking down the weed killer aisle at the store because of the smell. You can garden without it and, if you have kids, you should only garden without it because small hands will get into anything and everything. And small lungs are more susceptible to long-term detrimental outcomes that become autoimmune issues.

PERMACULTURE

Now what about permaculture? This book concentrates on organic permaculture practices to ensure that you have the best results for a healthy family garden. A healthy garden supports a healthy family. Permaculture supports a healthy earth as well. Permaculture means growing with nature, instead of going against it.

We will introduce several permaculture design methods to help you get in sync with the nature that is already all around you.

Greenhouses are a wonderful way to extend your growing season and control for pests and extreme weather conditions.

Tree frogs and birds are a sure sign of a healthy organic garden. They also eat harmful insects.

Annuals
constitute the
majority of the
vegetables
you get at the
supermarket.

Perennials and Annuals

Let's talk about perennials versus annuals. Which ones are you going to grow?

DO BOTH

Perennials are plants that come back every year and annuals are plants that start over every year. Depending on your zone, some "tender" perennials will act as annuals, in that they will die in a frost and have to be grown from seed anew every year or they can be overwintered in a greenhouse. Most of your garden variety vegetables and herbs are annuals.

Tomatoes, peppers, lettuce, basil, and cilantro are annuals. Perennials that come back every year will include your fruit trees, berry bushes, and some hardier herbs, like rosemary, lavender, mint, and lemon verbena. For a child-friendly garden that takes advantage of everything the world of edible plants has to offer, you will have both perennials and annuals. To determine which balance you want, take a look at your goals to decide if your goals for the first year are mostly short-term or long-term. Short-term goals might include getting your kids to eat veggies. That will place the focus on annuals.

GUILDS

Annuals have a great short-term turnaround. Some varieties of radishes are ready in 28 days. Long-term goals might include getting your kids to view gardening in a sustainable and purposeful way. This will take time and this is time that you can invest in perennials. One of my husband's favorite things in the world is the maple tree that he planted in his parent's backyard when he was ten years old. Now, 20 some odd years later, it is this grand, colorful specimen that we visit every time our son sees Bapa and YiaYia. As the saying goes, the best time to plant a tree was twenty years ago. The second best time is to plant one today.

Perennials form the heart of a growing guild. For the sake of quickness and convenience, the following plots (pg. 25) will aim at starting annuals so that you can get started on your growing journey with your family. If you have the resources to obtain fruit and nut trees, berry bushes, asparagus, or other long-term plants (aka perennials), then you can work on building a plant guild. I will also include one guild that you can use as a template for these projects.

If you have enough room, then you can plant rows of spinach, salad greens, kale, tomatoes, peppers, arugula, etc. Thirty inch rows, 30 feet to 100 feet long, are often used as a standard size because modern tillers and other garden machines span about 30 inches between their wheels. For a more modest garden (modest = manageable with children), 30-36 inch wide rows also work great because that is about how far you can reach to harvest or plant. On the next pages, we have rows that are 36 inches, but you can scale up to 48 inches or 4 ft. and you will still be able to reach into the middle for planting and harvesting.

∨∨ Your goals will feed directly into your balance of annuals and perennials. Annuals will reflect your short-term goals and most perennials will be long-term investments. Think what you want your children to learn today versus what you want them to know in the future.

Young orchard trees placed on drainage ditches, aka swales

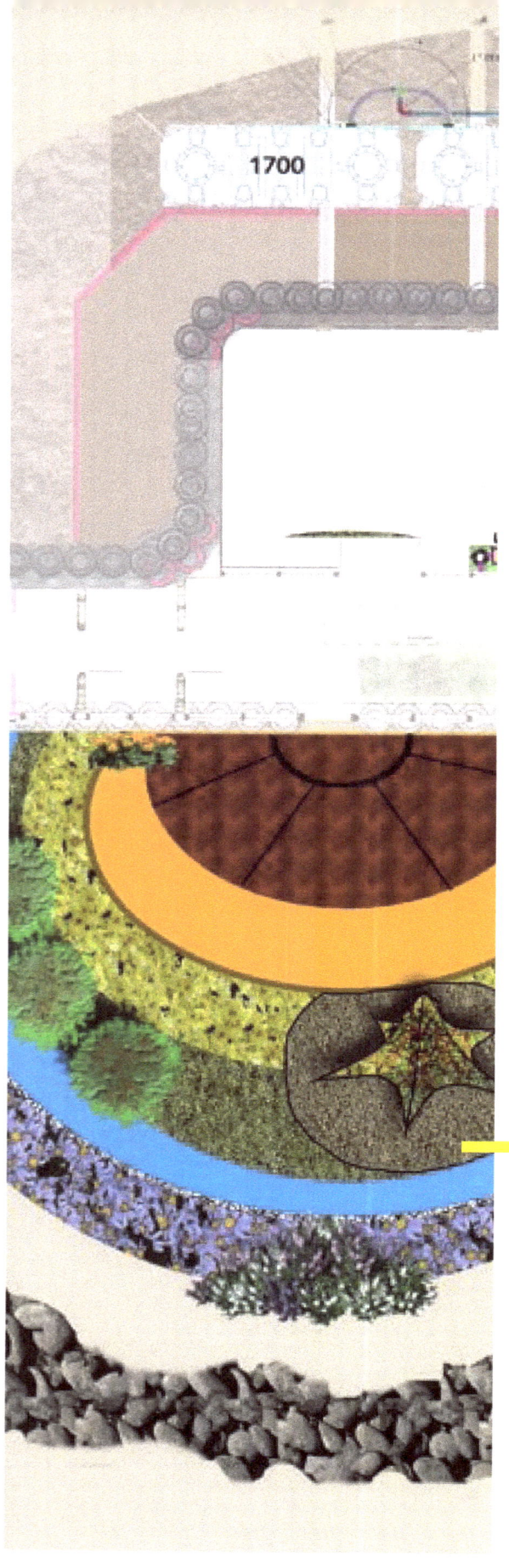

1700

No drawing
skills are
necessary to
design your
garden

Bam
a
a
b

Doub
Red
Oran

Yell
Gree

Blue

Purp

Deer
Purp

Quai

Mo
ne

02

Zones
Sector
Soils

The Plan

>>

You can also use Google maps to make simple shapes with measurements in feet or meters.

>>

Start thinking in zones when placing plants, trees, and shrubs. Zone 1 will be your kitchen garden and will be the best place for your herbs.

Soil Test

Organic Matter

Soil testing can also be achieved by taking a wet sample in your hand and squeezing it to see how much moisture it holds.

The "Soil Triangle" is published by the USDA. An ideal growing medium has a little bit of each, according to the type of plant that you are growing.

Soil Test Results

- 85% Sand
- 5% Clay
- 10% Silt
- Soil Texture Result
  - Loamy fine sand

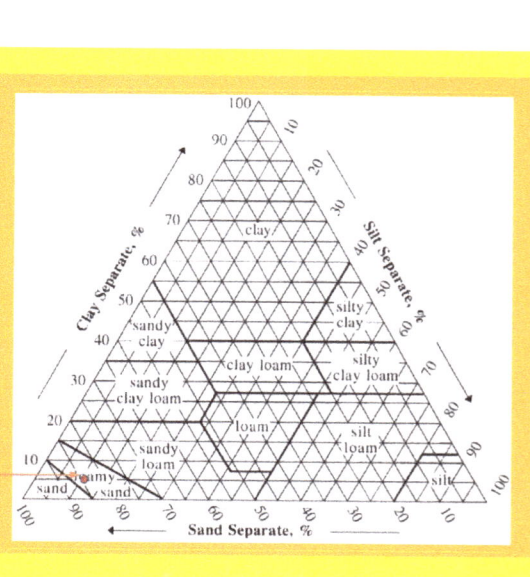

Permaculture Extra Credit: Looking at your Soil Makeup

Soil conditions relate to how much clay, silt, and sand you have in your soil. We also want to look at other factors, like is it really rocky?

In Tennessee, we are renowned for our rockiness and using raised beds have helped us out tremendously. If you do not know what kind of soil you have, you can perform a soil testing using a handful of your soil, water and a mason jar. Place soil and water in a jar, shake it, and let it settle for a few days. The different layers will separate according to density and then you can determine the percentage of each type of soil component.

The soil test from the Northern Nevada soil sample shown on these pages is mostly sand. To amend the soil and make it arable, several inches of compost were added on top of the sandy loam. Northern Nevada high desert is an unfavorable area for growing, but modern practices make it a possibility.

The Northern Idaho properties that we examined had better soil for growing, but ultimately had a less favorable growing season because of the short summers.

The middle Tennessee soils that we have looked at are largely variable. Some have been rocky. Some have been mostly clay. It is important for all regions to take a small assessment of where you are growing.

You can also look online at: https://www.nrcs.usda.gov/resources/data-and-reports/web-soil-survey

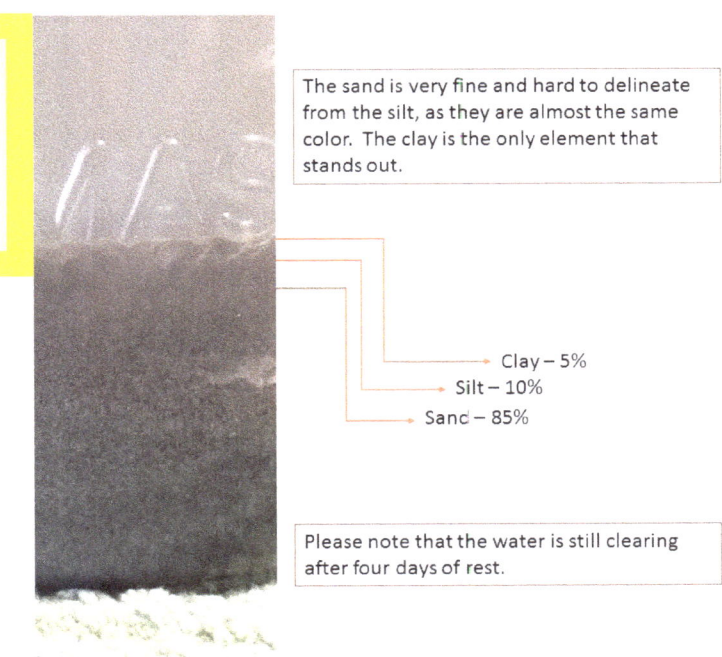

The sand is very fine and hard to delineate from the silt, as they are almost the same color. The clay is the only element that stands out.

Clay – 5%
Silt – 10%
Sand – 85%

Please note that the water is still clearing after four days of rest.

This website will bring up the soil survey for your area which provides a broad picture of your soil type. You can also download an additional pdf with specific information regarding whether or not your soil makes for a good growing situation. At the very least, it makes for a quick research opportunity for kids.

Raised beds filled with organic material covered in soil and compost will fix most problems. However, this will be at an additional cost. Your biggest ally in amending poor soil without raised beds will be time.

Being able to take an extra season to add wood chips or compost will greatly augment the moisture-retention ability and nutrient quality of your growing medium.

There is no perfect ratio for growing. Each plant has its individual requirements, but trying for equal portions of silt, clay, and sand is a good start.

Results from your local web soil survey will provide a starting basis for your soil amendment plan.

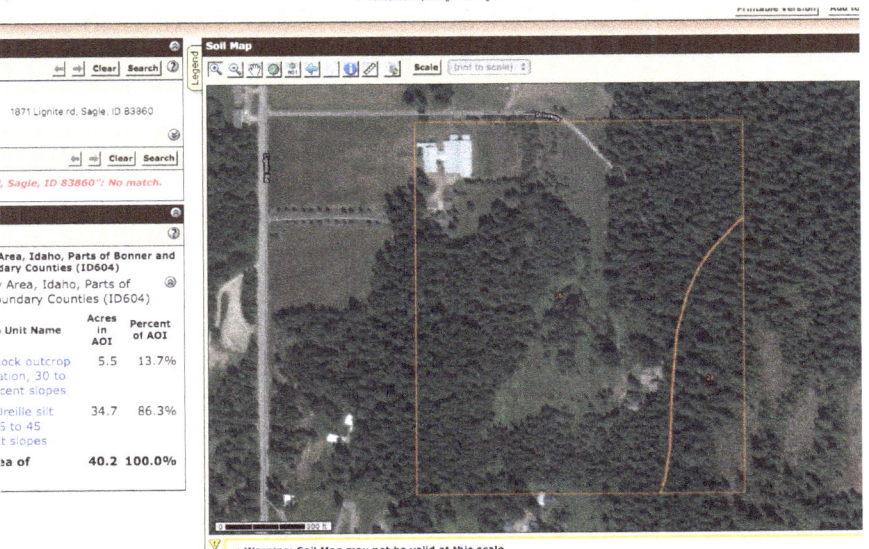

Warning: Soil Map may not be valid at this scale.

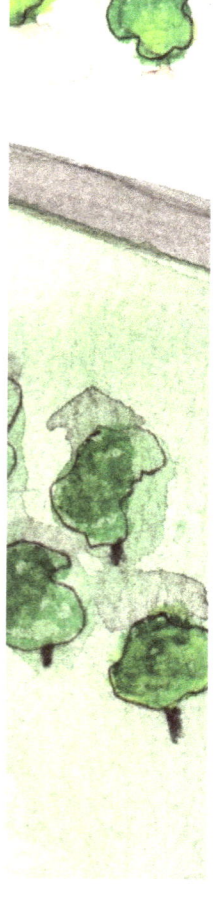

Now that we have our zones, sectors, and soil makeup. It's time for the plan, aka Fun Drawing Time! Don't let a lack of drawing skills psych you out. Circles, squares, and rectangles work just fine for figuring out where you will be placing your plants. I've included a few hand-drawn plans and a few easy computer drawn plans to get you started. You can also cut and paste with actual scissors and glue to move things around.

Time for the plan

Basic gardening needs to look at the position of the sun during the course of a day, flow of water, and soil conditions. These are you basic sectors. Zone thinking means that you will also place the most used plants or highest maintenance plants nearest your home.

These are the basics that you cannot overlook. The path of the sun during the course of the year will follow a southerly path. The height of the sun relative to your property will mean longer days, and more sunlight during the summer. Taking this into account, plant on the south side of your home or on the southern side of your backyard, if possible, and look at trees and fences as sun barriers.

Flow of water means looking at where water goes when it rains. Do you have a boggy area or "seasonal pond" that floods when it rains? Do you have a slope where soil will wash away? There are marsh-loving plants that you can grow for boggy areas. For slopes, you will want to even those out for planting which may require terracing, aka making little shelves to plant on. You can also use swales to direct the flow of water toward the roots of larger plants.

Your soil type will inform your garden design by suggesting in-ground growing, raised beds, or hugelkultur methods that we will explain later.

4 plots and a guild

Sample Plan On Facing Page

I am going to provide you with four sample plots that you can use or modify to your needs. These are based on a 3 x 3 ft. grid divided into 1 x 1 ft. blocks. Plot A (next page) shows two of the primary permaculture growing principles, interplanting and companion planting.

Permaculture supports a healthy earth as well.

Permaculture means growing with nature, instead of going against it.

Companion planting means a few things. It's not just that these plants are placed next to each other because they like each other's company. Tomato plants and basil support each other's well-being. Tomato finds basil to be amusing, but also supportive of tomato's goals and aspirations.

To be more scientific and more factually correct, the strong scent of the basil helps attract bees to the tomato plant's flowers which means a greater level of pollination for the tomato. Borage and marigold also attract pollinators, with the added benefit that marigold reduces root-knot nematodes in the soil. Marigold also attracts hoverflies which feed on white flies, one of your number one nemeses in the fight for tomato success (and goal aspiration).

Tomato	Basil	Tomato
Dill	Tomato	Borage/ Marigold
Sweet Pepper	Cilantro	Sweet Pepper

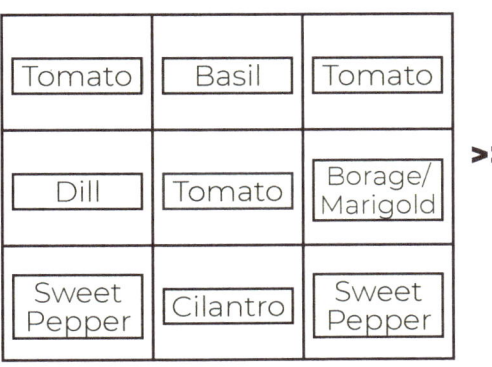

Plot A: Tomatoes Love Basil

Beans or Peas	Summer Squash	Beans or Peas
Corn	Corn	Corn
Beans or Peas	Summer Squash	Beans or Peas

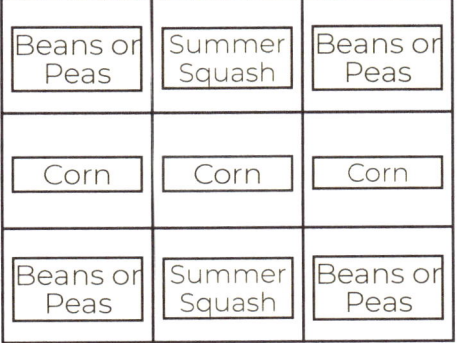

Plot B: Three Sisters

Fence line
N^
Plot A: Tomatoes Love Basil
Maple Tree
Plot B: Three Sisters
Herb Plot
House Exterior
Plot C: Brassica Land
Plot D: Pest Trap
Door
Lowbush Blueberries
Hostas
Hydrangea
Rhubarb

30 x 20 ft Backyard

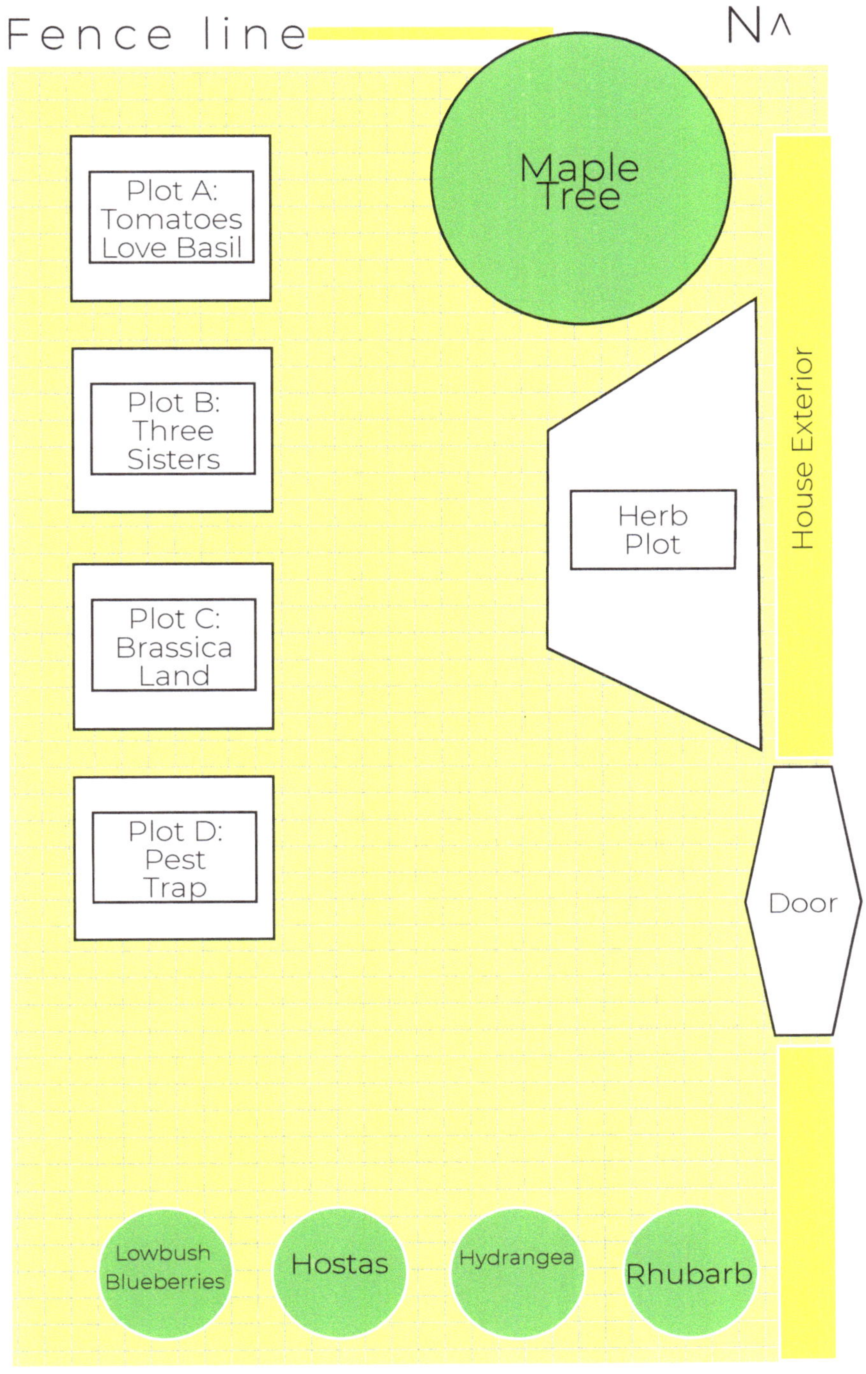

The seed inventory for Plot A is 4 tomato, 2 basil, 1 dill (young), 3 sweet pepper, 2 cilantro, and 2 borage or marigold seeds or starts. A small buffer has been added for these seeds. Plant the best sprouts and feel free to give away any that you don't have room for.

The "Three Sisters" planting option is a traditional method used by the Native Americans of North America. Plot B shows a central row of corn. Depending on the variety, you will direct seed the corn at 6 inches apart to start. After they have sprouted, you will thin to one foot apart. Beans are planted near the base of the corn. The corn stalk acts as a vertical support for the beans.

Summer or winter squash planted in the remaining space (remember that they will vine out to take up as much space as they can) will act as a living mulch to shade the soil and reduce evaporation. The beans or peas are nitrogen-fixers that grow up and around the corn. Nitrogen-fixing plants take nitrogen from the atmosphere and transfer it down in the ground to feed its neighbors and replenish nitrogen lost during the growing season.

Each level of the growing space is taken up by a plant and each plant supports the growth of the others. This is a true permaculture design. The seed inventory for Plot B is 16 beans or peas, 3 squash, 12 corn.

Time for the measuring tape. When you are recording your growing area make note of the sun, wet areas, and any existing features or plants that are already there, including where your windows are.

Brassicas, like broccoli, cabbage, and kale, do not get along with a lot of other plants. They also have different soil and watering requirements which mean that they should be grown separately from Plot A plants. The biggest factor for their growth is that they need a lot of space. If you have never grown brassicas before and you have only seen the end product at the grocery store, then you might be surprised by the large side leaves that they produce. On the other hand, kale is a little different because it is more of a vertical grower.

I placed two kale plants in this plot because you can harvest the leaves for a long period of time, which in my experience makes them more fun. The other brassicas in Plot C produce just one head and take a while to do that. They are great for learning patience and fortitude. They also make for a wonderful opportunity to splurge on starts just to make sure that you have the best beginning for your garden. One cabbage, 1 broccoli, 1 cauliflower, 3 kale make up Plot C. Grow one extra of the brassica of your choosing in case one of them fails to germinate.

Plot D is lovingly called a pest trap. You plant this plot a few feet away from your other plants and they draw the pests over to this area. Planting these plants earlier will allow time for the pests to find these plants first and, ideally, attract the predators for these pests. Aphids will be drawn to the early nasturtium, calendula, and nettle. Then ants and ladybugs will move in to eat these aphids. They will be in the neighborhood already

Cabbage		Cauli-flower
	Broccoli	
Kale		Kale

Plot C: Brassica Land

Nasturtium	Zinnia	Nettle
Radish	Dill	Zinnia
Calendula	Radish	Nasturtium

Plot D: Pest Trap
(Optional)

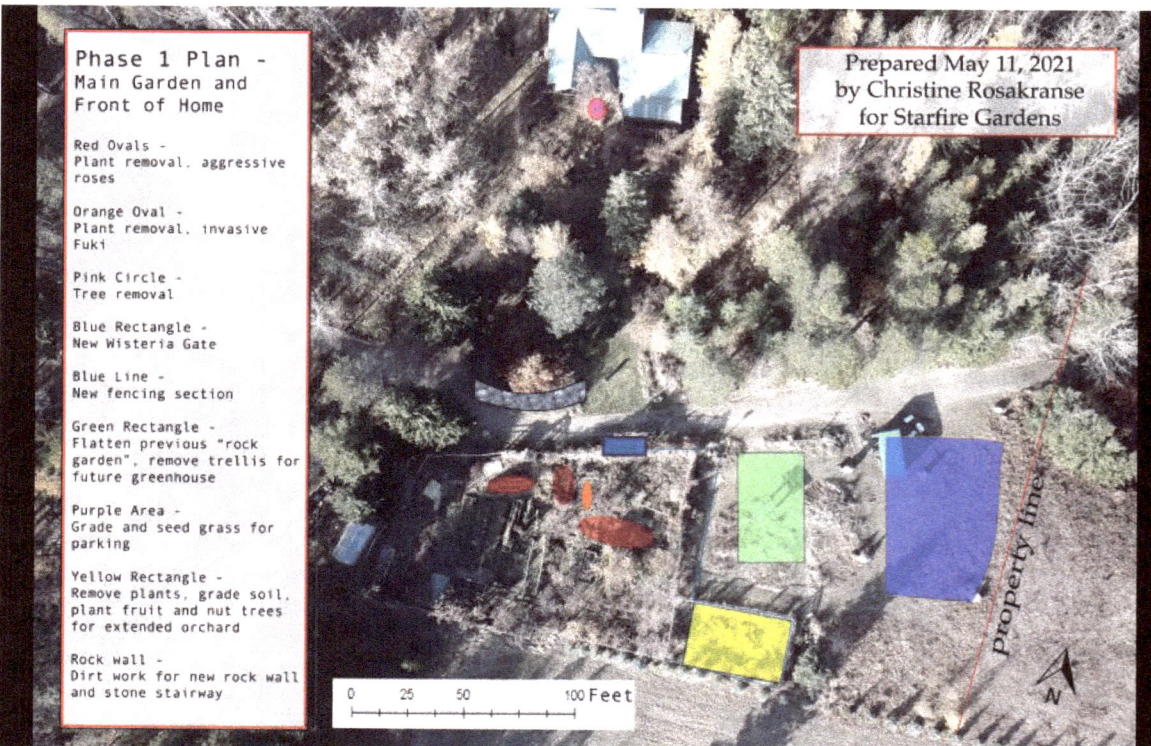

Phase 1 Plan -
Main Garden and
Front of Home

Red Ovals -
Plant removal, aggressive
roses

Orange Oval -
Plant removal, invasive
Fuki

Pink Circle -
Tree removal

Blue Rectangle -
New Wisteria Gate

Blue Line -
New fencing section

Green Rectangle -
Flatten previous "rock
garden", remove trellis for
future greenhouse

Purple Area -
Grade and seed grass for
parking

Yellow Rectangle -
Remove plants, grade soil,
plant fruit and nut trees
for extended orchard

Rock wall -
Dirt work for new rock wall
and stone stairway

Prepared May 11, 2021
by Christine Rosakranse
for Starfire Gardens

0   25   50   100 Feet

Feel free to use phases for your garden plan to indicate first steps versus long-term goals.

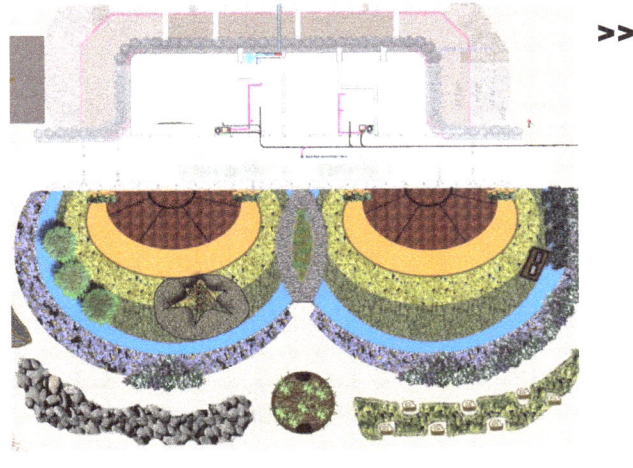

to deal with any aphids that land on your other plots when it comes time for them to sprout and grow. So the story goes.

The other type of "sacrificial" plant is one that just gets the daylights eaten out of it because the pests treat this like plant candy and devour it. Flea beetles won't have room for your cabbage because they are too busy filling up on radishes. Dill attracts the tomato hornworm moth and the moth will choose to deposit its eggs on the dill. Zinnia attracts the Japanese Beetle. When the zinnia is swarming with Japanese Beetles, pull up the whole plant and dunk it in soapy water.

Of course, you can also use pheromone bags for Japanese Beetle infestations. This invasive species will devastate a large variety of plants, so taking the steps to remove them completely might involve multiple courses of action. Seed inventory for Plot D: Pest Trap is 6 nasturtium, 4 zinnia, 1 dill, 1 nettle, 2 calendula, and 32 radishes (9-16 per square foot).

The next pages share a plant guild with you in case you want to try adding perennials into your basic garden plan.

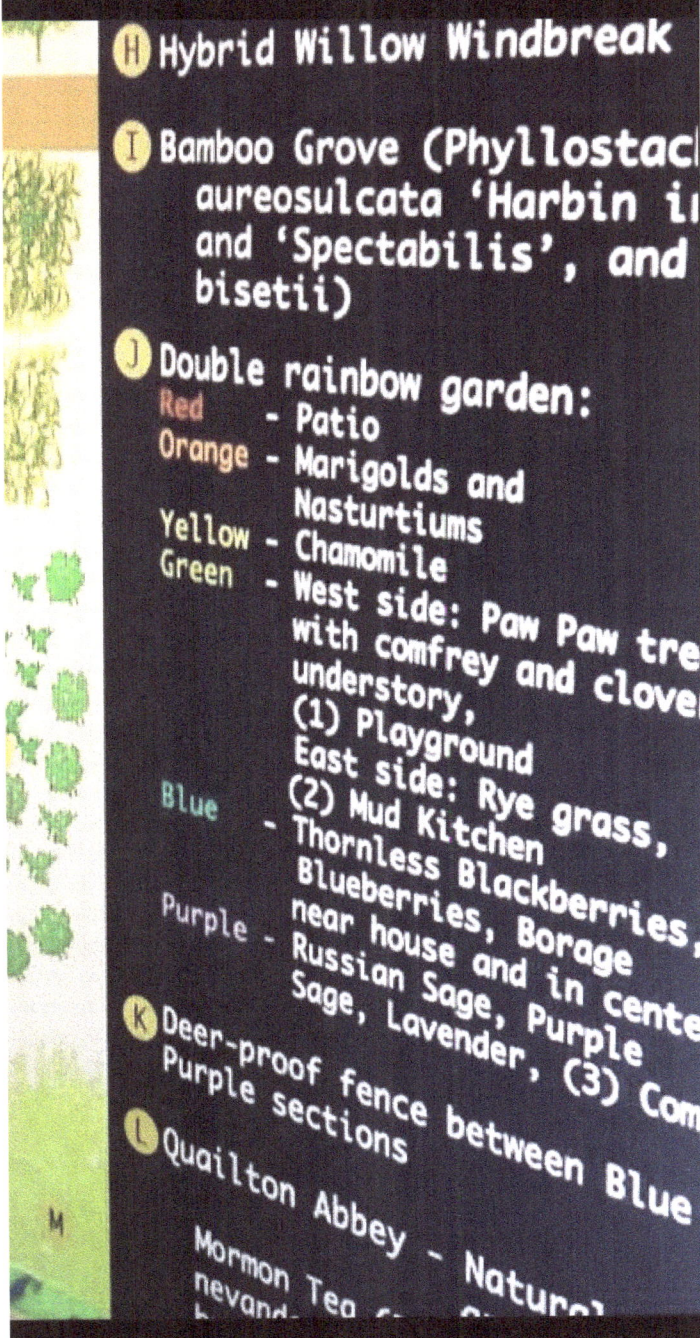

(H) Hybrid Willow Windbreak

(I) Bamboo Grove (Phyllostach aureosulcata 'Harbin i and 'Spectabilis', and bisetii)

(J) Double rainbow garden:
Red - Patio
Orange - Marigolds and Nasturtiums
Yellow - Chamomile
Green - West side: Paw Paw tre with comfrey and clove understory,
(1) Playground
East side: Rye grass,
(2) Mud Kitchen
Blue - Thornless Blackberries, Blueberries, Borage near house and in cente
Purple - Russian Sage, Purple Sage, Lavender, (3) Com

(K) Deer-proof fence between Blue Purple sections

(L) Quailton Abbey - Natural
Mormon Tea
nevand...

Sample garden plan for a Northern Nevada high desert plot with future earth berme home.

To make a basic plan, feel free to copy, cut, and paste the shared plots

>> Draw out your space and measure the room that you have to grow. If you have a large area, you might want to screenshot an overhead satellite view from an internet mapping application. For a 3 ft by 12 ft section, you can use one each of Plots 1-4. Feel free to copy and paste the seed inventory for each section as a buying plan.

The Plant Guild Story

Trying a permaculture approach in Northern Nevada proved to be challenging.

Once upon a time there was a cottonwood tree...

We have a number of cottonwoods on the property that run along a seasonal irrigation ditch. One cottonwood will be the base of the plant guild design. I have planted one cherry tree next to it (and there is another Bing cherry tree on the property for cross-pollination). We have at least one beaver and at least 40 deer that visit the property. We believe that the beaver lives under one of the dead cottonwoods on the ditch. The cottonwood is wrapped in chicken wire and the cherry tree has a cattle guard/fencing around it.

In order to add edible, medicinal, and other benefits to our homestead toolkit, I have selected borage, elderberry, lamb's ear, riparian grape, and daylily as the companion plants. The borage, elderberry, and daylily will reside primarily in the cattle fencing around the cherry tree. Over time they may come to sprout outside the fence to be pruned by the deer. The lamb's-ear was chosen because it is deer resistant, and as ground cover it may go beyond the fencing to visually unite the cottonwood area and the cherry tree. The riparian grape, while bitter and not usually used for human consumption, can provide food for the numerous bird species in the area, which in turn will provide food for the hawks we have on the property. Also, growing up the large cottonwood would preclude us from picking from the upper vines anyway.

All varieties were chosen for their ability to grow in our hardiness zone, with the water provided by the irrigation system, and in the soil that we have on the property near the ditch. It is hoped that introducing the borage and the fungal layer of mycorrhizae will build the soil health with mulch and additional nutrients. With the larger elements running parallel to the ditch and perpendicular to the southern sun, the understory should get plenty of light. We will maintain and trim the plants if they grow out of control.

Plant Guild Design

The Site

The Design

Key

Large Tree – Cottonwood
Small Tree – Rainier Cherry Tree

- Borage
- Lamb's-ear
- Elderberry
- Daylily
- Riparian Grape

*Ground inoculated with Mycorrhizae

Permaculture Plant Guilds

If you are growing for a family, as opposed to growing for a commercial business, and fun is one of your goals, then growing plants together in a symbiotic system called a guild is another way to go. Guilds use each layer of space to grow plants that complement each other in some way.

GUILD DESIGN

Back when we were starting a farm in Northern Nevada, we had a permaculture dream to grow around our enormous cottonwood trees. In this guild, we have lamb's ear, daylily, riparian grape, a Rainier cherry tree, and elderberry. Each of these plants have an edible and/or medicinal value, or they provide food for the local wildlife, including birds and pollinators.

The point of guilds is to utilize all of the possible growing space, including the vertical. You have a large tree, a smaller tree or bush, growing vines, medium-tall plants, and undergrowth plants. Thinking this way helps to adjust your plans to utilize what you already have in place. If you have a fruit tree already in your backyard, then you can think of guilds that you can grow around the base to support the tree and maximize the benefit of its shade. There are a few exceptions to this. Black walnut trees are allelopathic plants, which means that they secrete a chemical that makes it difficult for other plants to grow under them.

Maple trees tend to have shallow roots which makes it difficult to grow plants that need any soil to thrive. Pine trees change the pH of the soil which is growth prohibitive to some varieties of plant. There are a lot of varieties of flowers or flowering bushes that you can grow under pine trees, including hydrangeas, gardenias, and also ferns.

Before placing the plants that you want to grow on your drawing, take into account your sunlight in each area. Planting under trees or in the shade of a fence should be saved for shade-loving plants. You also have to take into account the type of tree as mentioned in the previous paragraphs, for pH and root growth habit.

Most vegetables and herbs will need full sun to grow, but you can grow mint, ginger, dill, and malabar spinach in more shady areas. You can also use fences to grow vines like peas or beans that might eventually reach the light. Passionfruit is also a vigorous grower, but be careful because it can overtake other trees and rob them of nutrition and light.

To plan out the individual plants, you can mix and match the plots above or just get out a pen and paper to draw something out less formally. There are, of course, computer programs dedicated to landscape design that you can use to plan your garden, but the investment of both time to learn and money to buy is not worth it for a family garden.

A hand-drawn placement of the tree guild plants with deer fencing.

As you see, you do not have to have artistic talent to make a quick sketch of where you want to place your plants

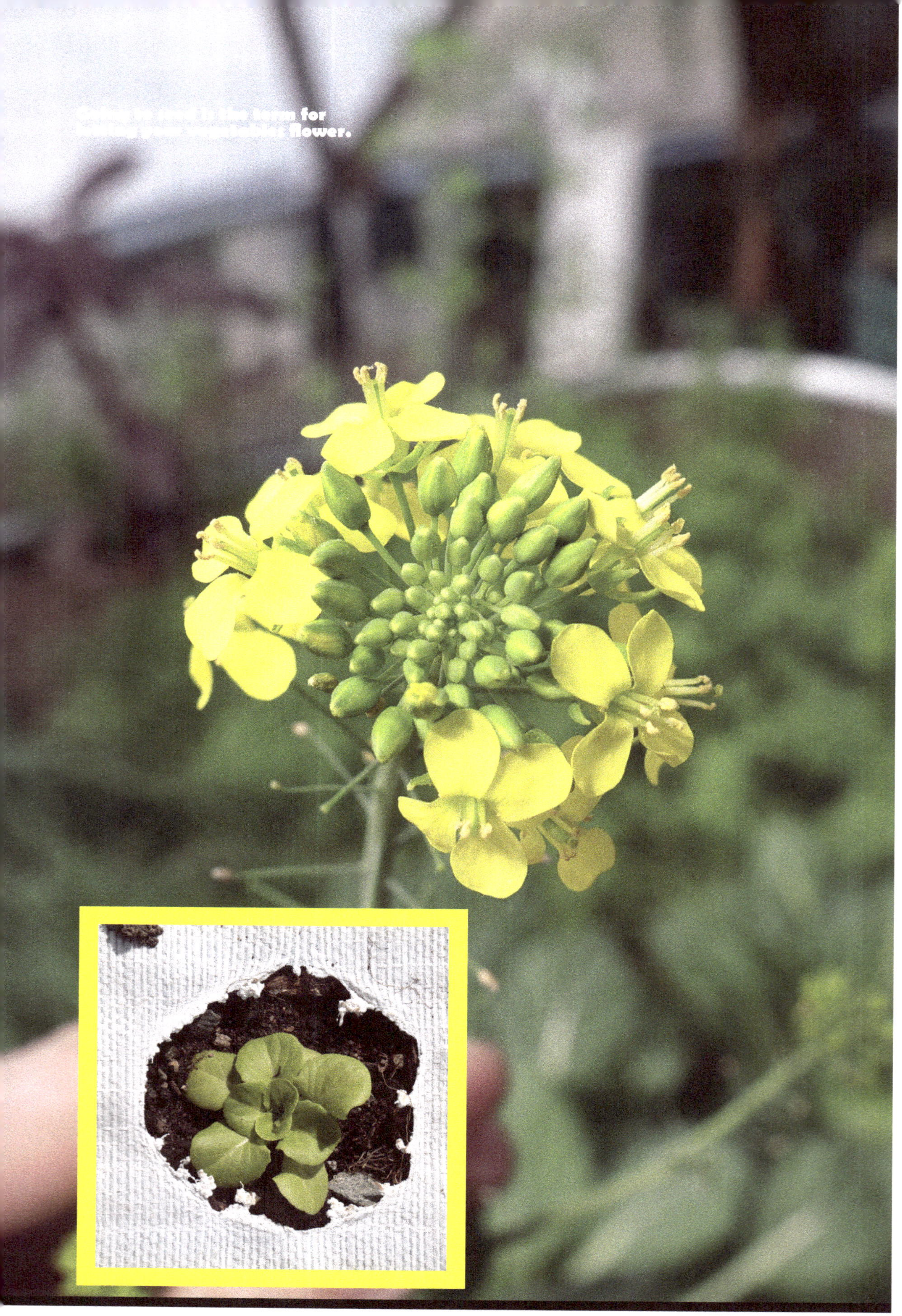

Going to seed is the term for letting your vegetables flower.

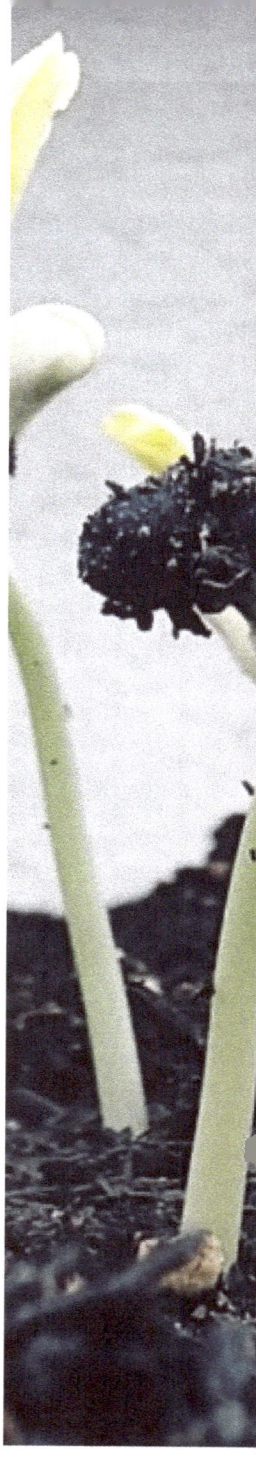

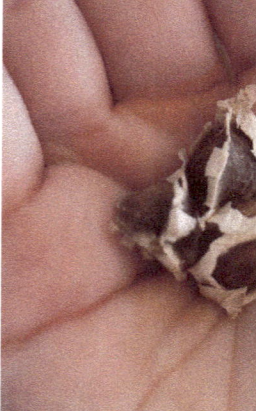

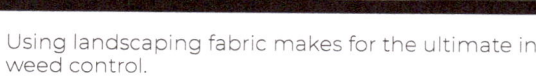

Using landscaping fabric makes for the ultimate in weed control.

03

Picking Out Seeds and Starting Your Garden Journals

Gita Pole Beans or any peas will grow up a trellis and make a great project for harvesting.

>> Can't we just get to planting already? Yes. Yes we can, but first, or third, we need the right supplies. These include seeds, soil, containers, and tiny gardening gloves and little shovels and just the cutest galoshes.

You might not need those last three things.

Some seeds are easier for small hands to place. These are moringa seeds.

Quick Side Note: You can either start your seeds or prep your space now depending on when you are starting. If you are starting January 1st, get seeds and then start them 6 - 8 weeks before your last frost date. If you are starting in the Fall of the year before, you will be preparing your space.

Time for the seeds

Let's talk about your main options of seeds versus starts. Seeds are going to provide your family with the best learning opportunities. You will need seeds to direct seed root veggies and some other items previously mentioned (garlic and potatoes). In the case of garlic, seeds will be cloves and, in the case of potatoes, seeds will be potatoes with eyes.

With seeds, you will learn more about the overall life cycle of each plant, including their germination and growth needs. "Starts" are already sprouted plants that take the guesswork out of some of the growing, but are going to cost more up front. They can range from 3-5 dollars each for annuals.

Professional growers add on 10% to the seed order to ensure you have enough even if you don't get 100% germination

For your initial foray into starting a garden, I would suggest you try both. Buy seeds and start them inside or direct sow, but also save some of the budget for a few starts. Treat yourself to items that are hard to start or use them as a backup if some of your seeds fail to germinate.

After you know where you are planting your vegetables, fruits, and herbs, you will want to make a list of how many of each type of plant you are planning to grow and where you want to plant it, if you have multiple locations. If you are using the plots as listed on the previous pages, you can cut and paste the seed inventory into a spreadsheet. In the spreadsheet provided here I have also included columns for direct seed versus transplant (DS or T), DTM or days to maturity, and when to seed for succession planting.

For those that are direct seeded, it can be quicker to do the math on what each square foot requires and buy that amount of seeds plus 10%. For radishes, you will have 9-16 radishes per square foot. For smaller plots, you will be hand seeding and the rate of planting will be more variable because you are eyeing your planting, unless you really want to use a ruler and measure out an inch between plants. For direct seeding where a lot of seeds are involved, you will buy in ounces versus a given number of seeds.

TRANSPLANT VS. DIRECT SEED

So now you might be thinking, when to transplant and when to direct sow? Growing from seed indoors and transplanting outside works well for most of the plants that you will be growing and it helps you to get a start on the growing season.

Tomatoes, cabbage, kale, lettuces, peppers, golden berries, and celery are all plants that you can start indoors and transfer out. Root vegetables, smaller baby lettuce mix varieties, garlic, and potatoes will all be direct seeded. You can see in the planting table that

Sample Seed Sheet

Plants to grow	DTM	# Seeds	Seeding	Transplant/Direct Seed
Arugula	35	72	4 (May 10, May 20, August 25, Sept. 1)	DS
Basil (Genovese)	68	72	1, transplanted May 20	T
Beet greens	40	1 oz.	Every 15 days, outdoors, from mid-april to	DS
Beets	60	1 oz.	6 (March 28, April 18, April 20, May 10, Jur	T
Carrots	85	1 oz.	8 (April 10, April 25, May 4, May 25, June 8	DS
Cilantro (Santo)	55	36	4/17, 5/15…..	DS
Cucumbers	50	72	2 (March 25, July 10)	T
Curly Kale (Westlander)	50	36	2 (April 10, July 1)	T
Flowers (Sunflowers, Lavender..)		3 pks		DS
Garlic (hard neck) x 1	N/A	150	Late October	DS
Garlic (soft neck) x 3	N/A	450	Late October	DS
Leeks	120	175	1, transplanted in early May	DS
Microgreens, Basil		1 oz.		DS
Microgreens, Cilantro		1 oz.		DS
Microgreens, Spicy Mix (Arugula)		1 oz.		DS
Mizuna (Red Kingdom, baby)	21	1 oz.	Every 15 days, outdoors, from mid-april to	DS
Parsley, Italian Flat Leaf	70	72	Starts May 1, 3 to 4 weeks before last frost	DS
Peppers	120	36	1, transplanted May 1	T
Radishes (French Breakfast, Red M	28	1 oz.	4 (May 10, May 23, July 11, August 20)	DS
Red Russian Kale (baby)	28	1 oz.	Every 15 days, outdoors, from mid-april to	DS
Romanesco		6	1, May 1st	T
Salanova Lettuces	45	1 oz.	Every 15 days, outdoors, from mid-april to	T
Spinach	45	1 oz.	4(April 1, April 25, July 25, August 5)	DS
Tatsoi, baby	21	1 oz.	Every 15 days, outdoors, from mid-april to	DS
Tomatoes, Granadero (Plum, Johnr	75	36	2 transplants, one in mid-April and one in i	T
Tomatoes, Sungold Cherry	57	36	2 transplants, one in mid-April and one in i	T
Zucchini (payload)	60	36	3 (April 4, May 3, June 20)	T
Delicata Squash	80-100	36	1 in May	DS
Pansies		1 oz.		DS
Amaranthus (love-lies-bleeding)	65-75	1/2 oz.		DS
Borage	90	36		DS

Salanova, a head lettuce variety, and kale are transplanted, while radishes, carrots, and baby kale are direct seeded. Leeks and onions, not listed, are started inside and then transplanted when they reach a certain height. So it's not an all allium are direct seeded sort of thing.

After you have your plant table prepared, you know how many seeds to order or how many starts to source. Professional growers add on 10% to the seed order to ensure you have enough even if you don't get 100% germination rate or if something else goes wrong.

You can always save seeds in a cool, dark space for a few years if you buy extra. You can also have a seed swap.

Planting sprouted potatoes in the spring

SEED TERMS

STRATIFICATION:
Some seeds need to experience a cold period in order to germinate.

SCARIFICATION;
Seeds need to be cut open a little to aid with germination

SEED SOAKING:
Using warm water to soak seeds for a short period of time aids germination.

FIRE-ACTIVATED:
Some seeds, like lodgepole pine and Eucalyptus, need to experience flame to sprout.

Seeds 101: The Basics

If you are growing less than 10 of any individual plant, then you may be buying more seeds than you need for one year. Depending on the variety, seed packs range from maybe 10 large seeds (mammoth sunflower or pumpkins) to 100 small seeds. For larger orders, you can buy in bulk and get it by weight.

If you do have extra seeds, you can swap them with another grower or you can save them. Properly stored, you can save seeds for a few years, though their germination rate will naturally decline over time. For example, if you originally bought seeds that were tested for a 95% germination rate, they will not maintain that ratio over time. This is

> You can also choose a regional company to purchase from because those seeds are biodynamically accustomed to your area.

why you might want to test old seeds by germinating/sprouting a handful of them before dedicating a large space for direct seeding.

You will also want to look at which seeds are easy to sprout versus which require certain steps that make them more difficult in general. Most seeds packets will mention as much information as possible, but looking online for information on rare or specialty plants will help you to pick the easier plants to grow.

SOURCING SEEDS

You can get seeds from a lot of places, including your local dollar store or large box store. For an organic garden, you will want to buy from a reputable source that produces non-GMO, organic seeds. Ideally, you want to get heirloom seeds especially if you want to save seeds from your harvest. Heirloom and organic do not mean the same thing. Organic is a growing practice and heirloom refers to plants that have been bred pure over several generations to ensure a certain characteristic, like color or drought tolerance.

For organic seeds, Johnny's Selected Seeds is a nationally renowned seed company. You can also choose a regional company to purchase from because those seeds are biodynamically accustomed to your area. Baker Creek and Snake River Seeds are two companies that serve the Intermountain Pacific Northwest, for example. Companies like these would have seeds that have survived the same drought or similar soil conditions that your garden has had and would therefore have seeds that are more suited to your region.

SEED SAVING

You can also save seeds yourself and who doesn't like free seeds? It's one of those things that we tend to overlook, but we have access to free seeds all the time! You can save seeds from store-bought vegetables and fruit. You can also save seeds from your own garden, but, of course, you have to have a garden started already and be at the end of the season for this. So, I will leave the details for saving seeds from your garden for the end of the book when it will be more applicable.

As for saving seed from store-bought fruits and vegetables, you cannot save seeds from every plant. Some plants are sprayed with chemicals to prevent the germination of the seeds. Some vegetables and fruits are hybrids that will not breed true to type, as opposed to heirlooms which will breed true. Some vegetables and fruits are also patent protected. So you have to be careful with these. How do you know if they are patented? You will sometimes see in seed, tree and starts catalogues plants that were bred by a certain facility or company and are patent protected which means that you are not allowed to propagate that plant from seed or cuttings. To avoid any difficulties, save seed from organic, heirloom, non-patented seeds whenever possible.

Now as to the varieties and types of plants that you buy from the store that you can save seed from - tomatoes, peppers, dragonfruit, winter squashes, and pumpkins make good seed saving projects. Tomato seeds have a jelly around them that you can wash away or get rid of by fermentation. Everything else on this list you can just wash and dry for later use. You might be asking yourself, but what about the other plants that you did not mention?

Some plants with seeds, even heirloom, organic seeds, are not suitable for seed saving because the seeds from a plant that are edible and sold in the store are not mature enough to be saved for later plantings. Okra, cucumbers, and summer squashes are usually left out in the field beyond their optimal eating time for the seeds to become larger and more suitable for saving.

EXTRA CREDIT PLANT RESEARCH

So we have talked a little about sourcir local seeds because they are most suite to your particular region. If you have th time and you have older kids, you migh want to research local, native species an figure out which ones are edible and/c medicinal. This sort of information wou be especially useful if you are attempting t create a permaculture guild garden plan.

After doing a little research, I discovere that Tennessee has a native passion-fru plant that they call Maypop. The fruit is nc very tasty, but it does have a beautiful flowe In Nevada, chicory grew in abundance an you can use the toasted roots as a coffe replacement.

When you research your native flora, you w find that you have free, robust edible anc or medicinal plants all around you alread Using these in a permaculture guild or a landscaping means that they will nee less inputs in terms of water, nutrients, an your time.

Other native flora that you might nc consider growing on purpose includ things like dandelion, which is actually ver nutritious. You might choose to leave thos kinds of helpful weeds instead of trying t get rid of them.

Feel free to use different phases for your garden plan to indicate first steps versus long-term goals.

Plant	Place in Food Forest	Attributes	Notes
Cottonwood – Populus fremontii	Tall Tree Layer	good for hugelkultur beds, can make fiber from the cottonwood "snow", good for boxes and baskets	Already on property, mature, 50 ft tall
Rainier Cherry Tree – Prunus avium	Low Tree Layer	edible fruit	We have two cherry trees already on property for fertilization. May try Paw Paw in the future.
Elderberry – Sambucus nigra	Shrub Layer	edible fruit and flowers, medicinal uses	
Borage - Borago officinalis	Herb Layer	pollinator plant, edible flowers, dynamic-accumulator (phosphorous), can fertilize and mulch, medicinal (borage seed oil)	Grows well and self-seeds
Lamb's-ear - Stachys byzantina	Ground-cover Layer	pollinator plant, medicinal (leaves are antibacterial, antiseptic, anti-inflammatory)	One planted already.
Riparian Grape – Vitis riparia	Vine Layer	edible fruit (but considered bitter), can be used for jellies and wine, food for birds, squirrels	Will grow up the Cottonwood
Daylily	Root Layer	edible, pollinator plant	
Mycorrhizae	Fungal Layer	Help with nutrient and water absorption	Forms symbiotic relationship with plants to "extend" root systems

Native plants shown above have multiple uses.

Introducing the Kid's Garden Journal

We are so close. Seeds are ordered. Garden Plan is designed. Maybe we started building some raised beds (you can skip ahead to the garden bed preparation section). I want to take a quick second to introduce the Kid's Garden Journal. Now that you know what seeds you are going to plant, you can start documenting your growing journey and the next two pages have a template you can use or modify to get started.

These pages have places for drawings or photos of your plant during its different growing stages. I also provided space for your inner scientist to geek out. What are the recordable data that will help us to improve our garden every year? The amount of detail will vary from child to child but pictures drawn with crayon can still convey a lot of information and the questions can spark more curiosity as to why things are the way they are.

>> **Take (and print out) photos or draw your seedlings and plants by hand. Feel free to try different drawing media to bolster your artistic confidence. Water colors and plant drawings do well together.**

Kid's Garden Journal

Plant Name:

SEEDLING

MATURE PLANT

FRUIT/ LEAF

Plant Name:

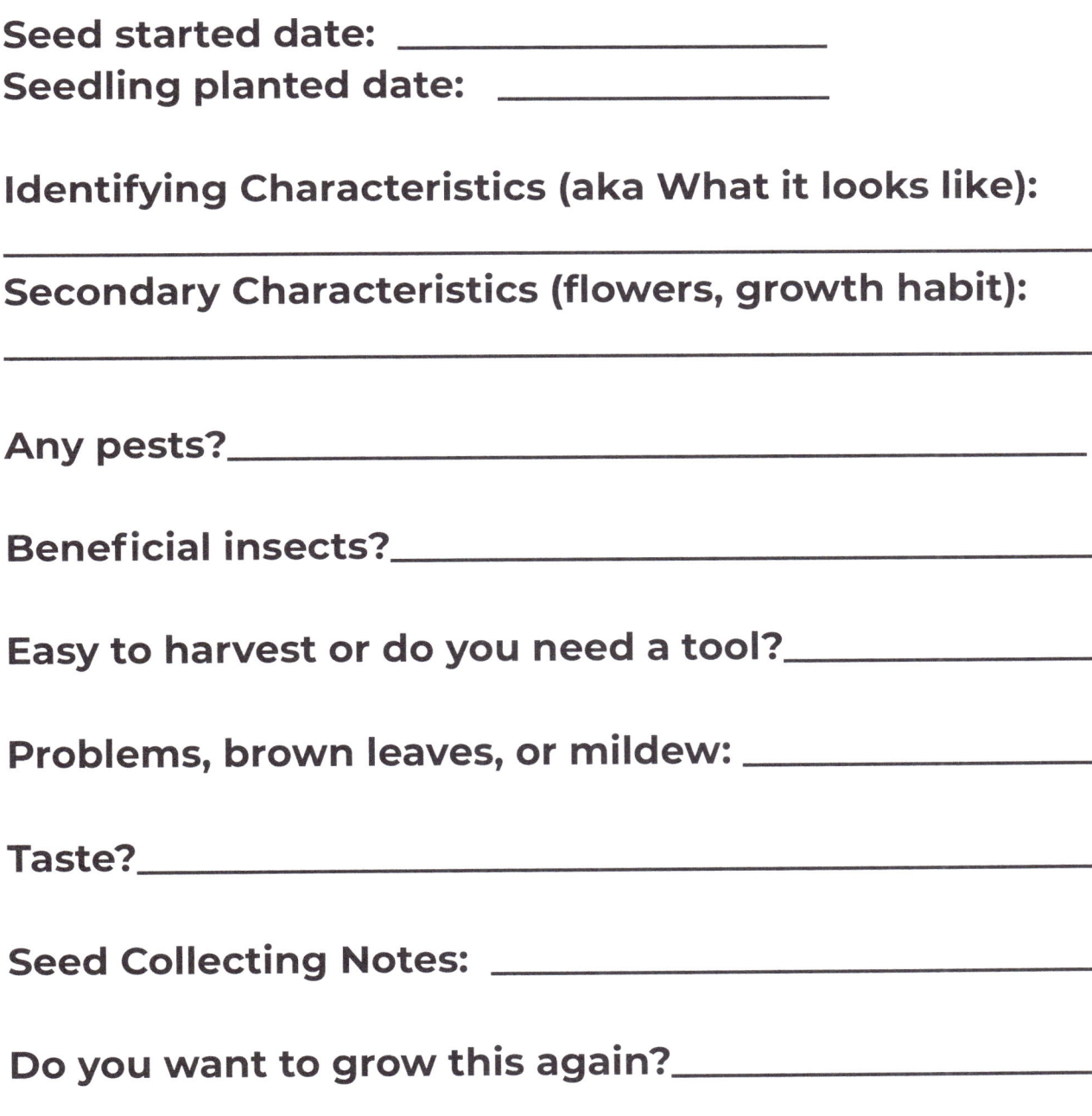

Seed started date: _____

Seedling planted date: _____

Identifying Characteristics (aka What it looks like):
_____

Secondary Characteristics (flowers, growth habit):
_____

Any pests?_____

Beneficial insects?_____

Easy to harvest or do you need a tool?_____

Problems, brown leaves, or mildew: _____

Taste?_____

Seed Collecting Notes: _____

Do you want to grow this again?_____

Favorite thing about this plant: _____

Side Note to Caretakers
KEEP NOTES TOO

When you are gardening, days and details go by pretty fast. Some plant might die at the beginning of your season, and you won't even remember that you planted it by the end of the season.

You will need to be keeping records too! Basically, you are looking at which plants you want to keep growing and which ones are giving you a hard time. Some plants that are not doing well might just need to be placed in a different area next year.

There are also so many fish in the sea! I mean, so many different types of plants that you can try. Use these journal questions to figure out what you want to grow again (save seed from), what you want to try again in a different place, or which ones you are just not excited about at all.

If you are dead set on growing a particular crop, try a different variety if the one you tried to grow did not work out.

Taking photos on your phone is also a great way to keep track of particular successes and problems. The additional benefit is that they have a time stamp, so you know which day you took the picture.

The Parent's Journal

(You can start a new list each time you go outside to check on your garden or you can keep a running list.)

Location of the plant:

Plant notes for each plant:

1. Easy to start?_____

2. Pest problems and type:_____

3. Yield good?_____

4. Growing problems:_____

5. Good spot for the plant? _____

6. Is it getting enough light, water, and nutrition:_____

Keeping track is one of the best ways to learn from your experience.

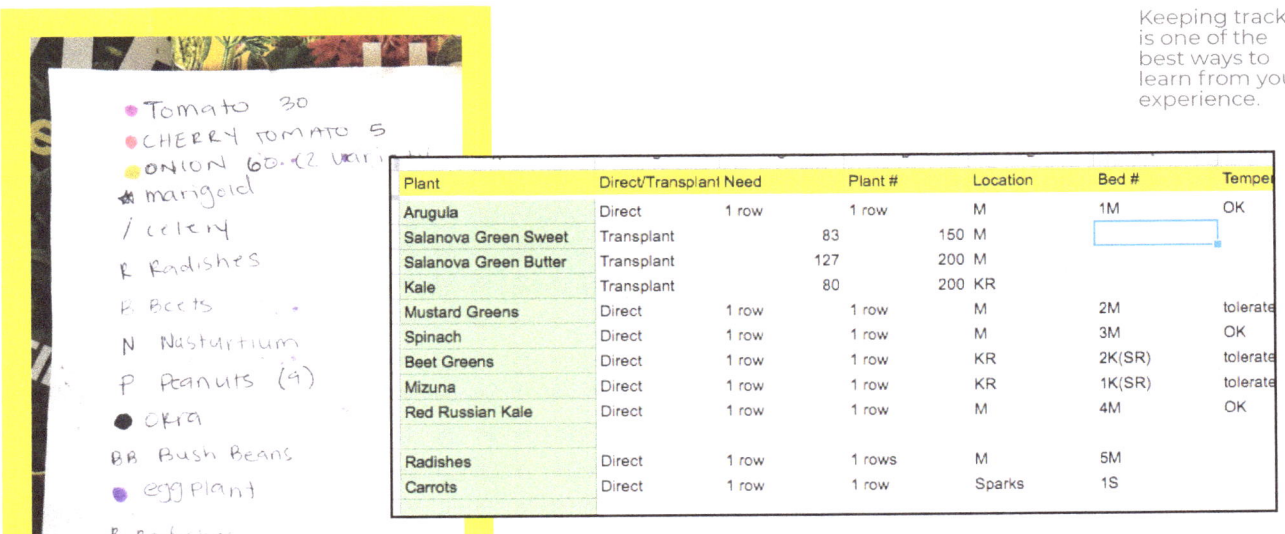

Plant	Direct/Transplant Need		Plant #	Location	Bed #	Temper
Arugula	Direct	1 row	1 row	M	1M	OK
Salanova Green Sweet	Transplant		83	150 M		
Salanova Green Butter	Transplant		127	200 M		
Kale	Transplant		80	200 KR		
Mustard Greens	Direct	1 row	1 row	M	2M	tolerate
Spinach	Direct	1 row	1 row	M	3M	OK
Beet Greens	Direct	1 row	1 row	KR	2K(SR)	tolerate
Mizuna	Direct	1 row	1 row	KR	1K(SR)	tolerate
Red Russian Kale	Direct	1 row	1 row	M	4M	OK
Radishes	Direct	1 row	1 rows	M	5M	
Carrots	Direct	1 row	1 row	Sparks	1S	

Handwritten list:
- Tomato 30
- CHERRY TOMATO 5
- ONION 60 (2 vari...
- marigold
- celery
- R Radishes
- B Beets
- N Nasturtium
- P Peanuts (9)
- Okra
- BB Bush Beans
- eggplant
- R Radishes

Seed selecting, collecting, and starting is the beginning of a life-long family adventure

04

Seed Sowing Basics: When & Where

>>

Get a container ready to moisten your seed starting mix, but be prepared for playtime toys getting in the dig site.

>>

Pick the right seed tray or container for your growing needs and the future needs of your plants.

Product Name	What is its use?	Supplier	What is the organic ingredient content?	If organic, who is the certifier?
Boost	Soil amendment	Full Circle Organic	100% organic	Bar-O
Punch	Compost tea	Full Circle Organic	100% organic	Bar-O
Soar	potting mix for seedlings	Full Circle Organic	100% organic	Bar-O
Cocotek	growing media from seedlings	General Hydroponics	100% organic	OMRI
Dr. Earth 733 Organic 5 Fertilizer	for tomato, vegetable, herb	Dr. Earth	100% organic	OMRI
Organic Perlite	improving soil	Espoma	100% organic	USDA
Worm Castings	soil amendment	Unco Industries	100% organic	OMRI
Organic Vermiculite	soil amendment	Espoma		USDA

Sample organic inputs including soil, growing medium, and fertilizer.

These Winstrip brand trays are easier to pop seedlings out of, but 6 cell trays are more convenient for smaller gardens with fewer plants.

eeds starting mix ften has higher eat moss or coco oir content.

When it comes to ontainers, you do ou boo! Or rather, ollow your budget. ust make sure our containers ave holes for rainage.

Seed Starting

GET SEEDS ACCORDING TO YOUR PLAN

You have your plan, right? It doesn't have to be in a spreadsheet, but you need something. Order your seeds according to your plan, adding a ten percent overage for larger batches of plants. Try to order them as soon as you have your plan so they come in time for an early spring planting.

GERMINATION

For most seeds, germination is pretty simple. If they came in a seed packet, then the sowing instructions will be on the back of the packet. This will tell you what depth and what temperature of soil to aim for when you are starting your seeds. Some seeds require extra steps, like scarification, stratification, or sprouting on a wet paper towel. For example, lavender requires cold stratification which means that you have to place it in the refrigerator for a few weeks before you sprout them. Moringa seeds have to be soaked in warm water for 2-3 days prior to planting. Andrographis should be soaked in 120 degree water for five minutes before sowing.

These extra steps are fun learning opportunities and make for great party

Milk jugs makes wonderful mini-greenhouses that you can start seedlings in during the end of your winter for a jump on the season.

conversation, but if you want a more fool-proof growing process, then you might want to skip some of the more difficult-to-start varieties or any plants that take years to mature.

Use a high quality organic seed starting mix. These mixes tend to have more peat moss or coconut coir to retain moisture to help the seed stay moist to encourage germination. In the table on the opposite page I am including our full list of organic inputs.

While you are out purchasing or sourcing growing medium, you might also want to be on the lookout for garden soil and fertilizer that you will need further down the gardening adventure road.

Get growing trays, small pots, cups, or milk jugs?

Select a growing container to fit your seed needs and budget. If you are seed starting indoors, you will use trays with individual cells, small pots, plastic cups or yogurt containers. The size and type of the container will depend on the seed that you are trying to start. For most seeds, you can use a smaller cell and pot them up to a larger size if need be. For some, you need to start with a

larger container because they don't like to be moved and have their roots disturbed or they grow deep roots before you can move them outside. This pertains to plants like echinacea, with a 3 inch deep taproot, and cucumbers, with tender roots.

If you would like to start seeds outdoors, you can repurpose milk jugs or water jugs to make individual greenhouses. First poke holes into the top for watering and into the bottom for drainage.

Then cut the top off about ⅔ of the way down the jug, below the handle, leaving a little piece connected to act as a hinge. Then place moist soil in the bottom part, sow your seeds as you would normally, close the hinged top with duct tape or wire, and place outside in an area that gets light. More kid-centered sowing seed directions are provided in the sowing seeds section.

The duct tape will sometimes unglue itself or become difficult to stick back on, so you can use a little wire loop to connect two holes in the top and bottom located on the opposite side to the hinge. The top acts as a greenhouse to protect the seeds from freezing. Some plants prefer this method of germination if they require cold stratification. You can actively cover and uncover the seedlings if it is getting too hot or cold before you plant them in the garden.

For indoor growing, If you are growing a large number of any seed, as in a commercial production, you will use trays that have 36, 72, or 128 cells. However, for your average home

growing situation you will want to use smaller trays. Six cell trays that fit into a larger base tray will allow you to germinate 6 of the same type of plant and then move them out when they are ready to transplant. If you use a 72 cell tray and try to grow many different varieties of vegetables and herbs that sprout at different times or that require different levels of attention, you will not be able to necessarily get the best results. I've had difficulties trying to pop out one row while leaving the others intact. Some trays have pretty large holes on the bottom, which make popping out all the soil blocks easier, but also make popping out one row pretty messy.

It's doable, but you can save some grief by using the 6 cell packs or individual 3 inch pots. If you want to grow less than six of any plant in the 6 cell packs, then just try to put "like" plants together with similar germination times and requirements together. This also holds true for placing multiple varieties of plants in the same 72 cell tray. What might your requirements include? Some plants like warm soil for germination. Some need cooler soil. Some plants like a lot of water or moisture. Some do not like having "wet feet". Some need light to germinate. Usually this will mean just placing the seed on top of the soil and tamping it in a little bit. Some only germinate in darkness. They will be planted at a certain depth, but you would cover some of them with a tray to prevent all light from getting to them.

For example, you can have three tomatoes and three peppers in the same tray or three basil plants and three dills. They all need the same amount of water, heat, and light. You can also grow in individual 3 inch pots to get around the problem of needing similar germination times. This works well for larger plants that you don't want to "pot up" before their final move to the outside. This size container is what you commonly see for sale in garden nurseries.

GROW LIGHTS OR NO GROW LIGHTS?

If you have a south-facing window with a shelf or table in front of it, you can get away with not having lights.

WHITE LED SHOP LIGHTS...

can be the solution to your problems if you have a small space, kids, cats, or lack a south-facing windows.

They do not emit enough heat to need a fan and they work just fine for starting seeds. You are not growing for a fancy flower show.

If you have a dedicated greenhouse, you can get away with not having lights. If you are using the milk jug method, you will not need lights. But setting up lights on a shelving unit is easy and it gives you many more options as to where you can put your growing setup as long as you can run a power cord to it. You can keep it in a closet with no windows at all if you need to.

Lights on a shelving unit can help in situations where you have cats or other animals that might mess with your seed trays or soil. I started peonies indoors one year and quickly learned that my cats loved to use the large pots of soil as their urinal.

It can also help if you have small children. You can place lights higher up on the shelves and keep them away from little hands. If you have a north facing window, light are necessary to augment the light that your seedlings get.

We use a wire shelving unit from a big box store like Costco or Target and two four foot long LED shop lights for each shelf. White LEDs work fine and they don't get hot, so you don't need additional ventilation or fans to make sure that you are not burning your plants. We also have lights with certain colored bulbs that are supposed to help with growing and flowering, but for a smaller home garden this is not necessary. Some of them can also be loud because they do have integrated fans. I am including a picture here of both our normal setup and the setup with red grow lights. The one with the red grow lights is more of a friendly reminder to not start your plants too early or you will have 6 ft tall tomato plants before your husband has finished building the new greenhouse. Just saying.

Six foot tall tomato plants inside are a big oops. We started them way too early due to delays in greenhouse construction.

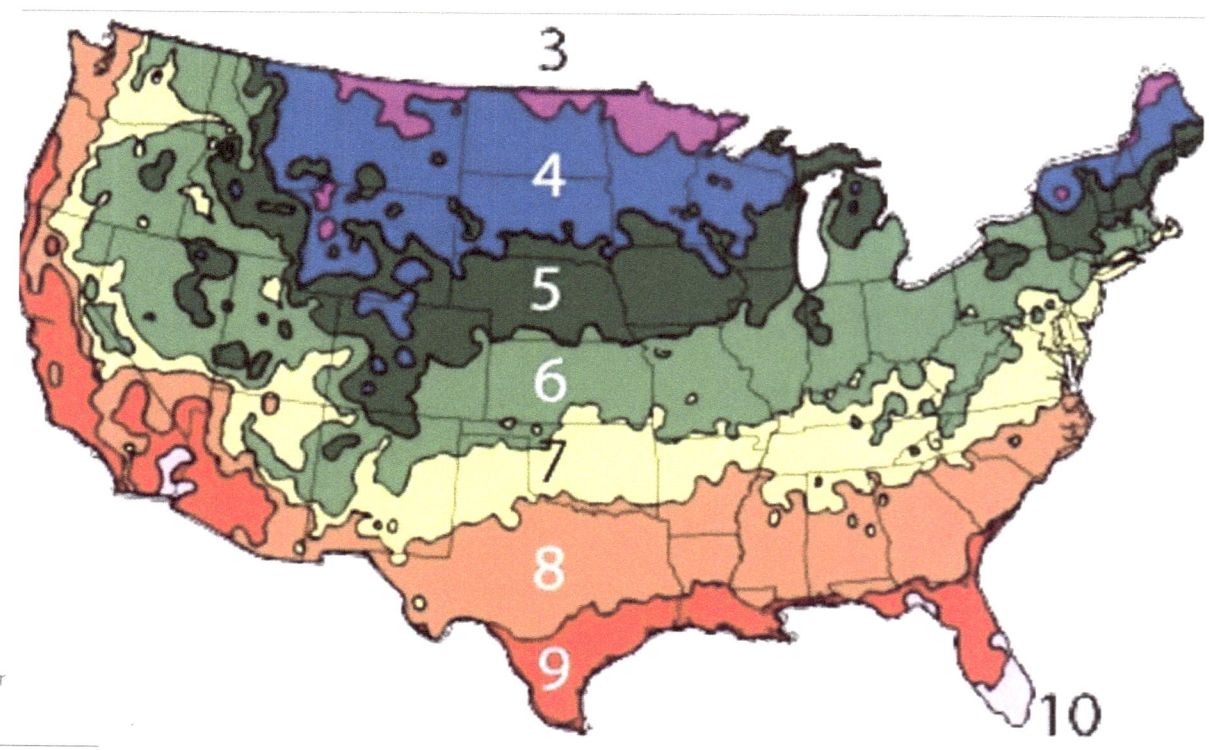

USDA Plant Hardiness Map shows how cold it gets for a particular region

The shop lights can be connected in series, plugging one into the other so you will not necessarily need additional power strips. You will also want to get a timer for the lights. Set it to 12 hours or whatever your seed packs recommend. You can also buy seed mats that keep the trays warm (around 72 degrees) if you are growing certain plants, especially flowers, that need warmer soil to germinate.

FROST DATE

You have your seeds, soil, containers, and growing area set up. If you started the new year with growing in mind, you will want to start your seeds about 6-8 weeks before the last frost date. If you don't know when that is, go to the USDA plant hardiness zone web page (USDA Plant Hardiness Zone Map) and enter your zip code. This will give you your growing zone. Then look up "frost date" and your zip code and you will find that last date of the year that you may get frost or the temperature will drop below freezing. For zone 6b in Tennessee, this is April 15th.

USDA Hardiness Zone and your last frost date are not interchangeable information. You have to know both in order to anticipate the length of your growing season and the intensity of your cold during the winter. Some zones will not have a long enough growing season to grow certain vegetables and fruit unless you have a greenhouse. Golden berries, for example, have a very long growing season and cannot freeze and recover. They are therefore considered tropical (Zone 9-11) and will not be able to bear fruit in more northerly zones.

You have to know both your USDA Hardiness Zone and your last frost date in order to plan your garden.

A small greenhouse is Northern Nevada designed to prolong the growing season.

>> **Don't start any plants that require a longer growing season than you are able to provide. Looking at what growers sell at the local farmer's market will give you a good indication as to what grows well in your area.**

Peas are a very satisfying early starter for your organic family garden. It's also a fun activity to plant them and watch them grow up a trellis. Sugar snap peas and snow peas can be eaten directly from the garden.

Sowing the Seeds (Of Love)

Now it is time for the fun part! Sowing seeds is always a enjoyable time with the family. For those with younger children, it is helpful to know ways to help keep it pleasant. Number One: place moist dirt into containers outside if you can. Young kids are great at filling up containers with dirt. They are natural experts. They are not so great at not getting that soil everywhere.

After the dirt is in the trays, pots, cups, or jugs, if you have not moistened the soil beforehand, soak them with water before planting the seeds. Pre-soaking can also be part of the fun. Just be careful with the volume of water because a well placed spray can knock all the soil out of a pot.

Okra seeds, pelleted carrot seeds or lettuce seeds, peas, beans and squash seeds are the big, beefy deals that little hands can easily grab.

Some seeds need sun to germinate and you will just be placing those on the soil surface and maybe lightly dusting them with soil. For all the others you will have a certain depth for planting. You can make the holes with the back of a sharpie or other pen. Just go down to an inch or ½ inch or whatever your seed packet says. Older kids will be able to do this just fine. With younger kids, it is your judgment call. My little guy loves to make the holes. I just adjust the depth afterwards by taking away or adding soil on top. You now have soil in the containers, you have watered the soil, and you have little holes of the approximate required depth.

Now it is time to sow your seeds. Once again this depends on the age of your child and their level of manual dexterity. Okra seeds, pelleted carrot seeds or lettuce seeds, peas, beans and squash seeds are the big, beefy deals that little hands can easily grab. They take one seed (or bean) and place it in the dirt. Cover it with soil, water again. Easy, peas-y. Though beans like to be belly down in the dirt, so take note.

Other seeds range from small to teeny-weeny. If they are small, then you might take the seed packet or even smaller inner envelope and gently pour the seeds, using a slight shaking to get them to the edge of the packet. You can also use specialized seed-pouring devices that have certain size

Your dirt tray or bin may end up becoming a construction zone for small backhoes and excavators.

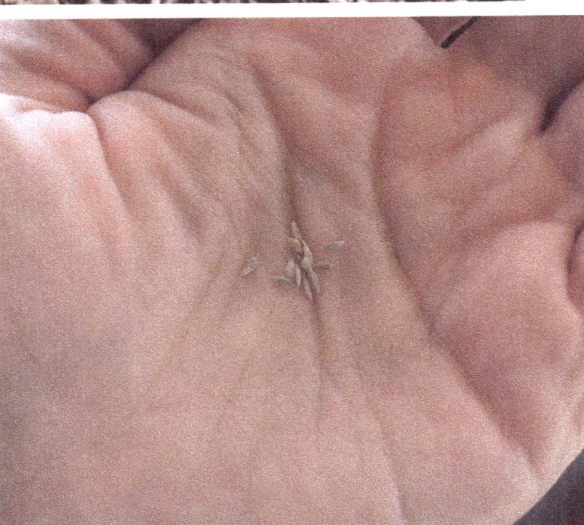

Some seeds are eenie-weenie. Some seeds are big, beefy deals. Choose which ones you sow with your children accordingly.

holes to permit a certain number of seeds to pass. Or you can use a spoon.

After one type of seed gets placed, you will want to label them with a tag. You can buy labels, use popsicle sticks, or cut yogurt containers into strips. You will then use a permanent marker or paint marker to write the name of the plant and, if you are fancy, the date of the planting. If you use popsicles, the lettering might bleed, even if you use a permanent marker. Take your label and jab it into the container.

You don't need one for each container. You only need one for each type, but you have to figure out how you are keeping track. You can reuse these labels when you plant the seedlings out into the garden. Or you can make nice big signs from tree bark, wood, paint and screws like we did for our garlic plot. Fun project alert!! See insert on opposite page.

AFTER SOWING YOUR SEEDS

Depending on the variety of plant, some seeds will take 4-8 weeks or more to germinate and pop up above the soil line. Some will only take a few days. Once again, the seed packet will tell you and if it doesn't the internet will. You will be watering them regularly so they don't dry out. Outdoor jugs will get natural light. Indoor starts will get light from a south-facing window or from white LED shoplights. Some, like lemongrass, will prefer a very moist growing environment, so you can cover those with a glass or plastic dome, or use clear wrap to keep them moist.

Given enough time they will start sending roots out of the growing container that you have put them in. If you timed it right, seeing roots come out of the bottom of the container will coincide with your last frost date and you can just place them in the ground. If they are too root-y or root-bound before your last frost date then you will have to up-pot or pot them up.

That simply means that you will move them from a smaller container to a larger container. You will add a little soil to the new container and then pop it over, taking care to fill in the sides and water in.

You will want to help the younger kids with this because some plants can be brittle, meaning that branches or stems will pop off if

Homemade plant signs are a fun way to get your kids excited for the future.

>>

you look at them the wrong way. Others do not like being messed with at all!! They will totally be all like, "Ouch, my roots!" Cucumbers are like this. I'm not calling them the Karens of the edible plant community, but maybe they are.

Most plants are pretty sturdy. Remember, they want to live! Just have the right tools and know-how to give them the best chance. Turn the pot on its side or use a butter knife to help wedge the seedling roots out of the tray. Also, stack the deck in your favor with hard to kill varieties, like tomatoes.

Tomatoes can be planted deep, well beyond their first leaves. We will call them the anti-Karens. They are cool. Even though they are determinate or indeterminate. Did we talk about that yet?

SIDE NOTE ON TOMATOES

Determinate versus Indeterminate

Yes, there are two types of tomato. Determinate is a bush type and indeterminate is a vine type, which will produce more tomatoes, but it will require trellising. You need to be able to train it on an upright structure. Cattle panels work if you can clip them in. Otherwise, you can have two T-posts at the end of your row and run string down from a central wire.

>> **There are no failures in growing, only learning opportunities. I know it sounds hackneyed or old-fashioned, but you have to adopt this viewpoint if you are going to keep everything fun for your kids.**

A double rainbow.
You will find all sorts of
surprises pop up when
you are outside more.

Raised beds are a
wonderful option, but
they can be costly for a
new gardener.

05

Preparing Your Growing Space : The Options

>> Alright, seeds are started! (Or not and you have skipped ahead in the book to accommodate your season).

And wasn't that so much fun. A few of them have even popped, like the sugar snap peas and snow peas. Dianthus, mint, basil. You have a little while until your last frost date, so now is a great time to prep the garden space if you haven't already.

A tilther works well for integrating top compost or fertilizer into the underlying soil.

Raised bed make it easier to grow in rocky soil.

What is your soil situation?

>>

Your soil situation will dictate how you need to grow, be it in a raised bed, in containers, or in the ground. Take into account that setting up a growing space is a long-term investment, but one that can be made over the course of years.

Now is the time for honesty. Ideally, you would have laid out a tarp or started with "lasagna" mulching last fall. Tarping allows weed seeds to germinate, start to grow, and then be killed because they can't get sun or water, only the heat of the day through the tarp. You can leave the dead material where it lies or chuck it into the compost bin.

"Lasagna" mulching uses layers of cardboard to smother the weeds underneath, but the cardboard and additional compost also need time to break down and add nutrients, like nitrogen and carbon, back into the soil. Both of these methods take time. Hopefully, you tarp for at least 3 months and "lasagna" mulch for 6 months. So what if you didn't have time to tarp or "lasagna" mulch?

OPTIONS

You have a few options. Some are more fun than others, and some are more kid-friendly than others. You have a patch of soil out back, just so happens to measure 3 x 3 ft. You can plant right into the ground, make a hugelkultur mound, grow in straw bales, or you can make a raised bed.

I will assume the terms in-the-ground, straw bales, and raised bed are pretty straight forward, but perhaps you have not heard of hugelkultur before. Hugelkultur involves making a long mound built from several layers - with large wooden rounds in the middle, topped with smaller branches, topped with straw, then topped with soil and mulch.

Each approach has pros and cons. The main trade off is money and time. Raised beds are not free. Not only do you have to buy the materials to make the raised bed, but you have to purchase soil to fill it.

Depending on the depth of the raised bed, this can add up. However, if you think of them as a long term investment, then you can rationalize the cost. You can also utilize hugelkultur techniques to fill some of the raised bed with branches and wood rounds to take up space and increase the biodynamics of the soil structure.

If you are renting, you might not want to go the raised bed route unless your landlord would reimburse you. If you are being budget savvy or if you are growing over a large space, then growing in the ground will appeal most to you. Hugelkultur and straw bales form the middle ground by using freely available natural resources to raise your growing surface and provide structure for your growing space. Not all plants are suited to hugelkultur or straw bales, however. Hugelkultur mounds also take time. Ideally, your hugelkultur mound has a few months to settle in before you plant into it.

There are other options as well, including hydroponics and aquaponics, but neither of these are really entry-level hobby gardening projects. So let's look at raised beds versus in-ground growing.

Poor alkaline soil in Northern Nevada meant a lot of amendments to the soil.

We are going to present three options for growing, but a lot of the methods for weed prevention, amending the soil, and dealing with pests will be the same. Some of these topics will be covered later in the maintenance section.

Option 1: In-ground Growing

In-ground growing, if you have not had time to tarp or "lasagna mulch", involves taking care of the weeds, large rocks and debris, and amending your soil for optimal growth.

WEED PREVENTION

First, you will want to mulch or use weed barrier fabric for a number of reasons. The main reason is weed prevention. A thick layer of mulch or a weed barrier fabric will block light and smother weeds. You can make holes in weed barrier fabric to fit your seedlings.

After mulching, you would just pull back the mulch from where you are planting and insert the seedlings. If you are direct sowing, like you would for radishes or baby greens, you would only use mulch or barrier fabric between your rows where you want to walk. Flame weed before you plant helps kill anything you don't want popping up in your radish rows.

Mulching with wood chips, wood bark, straw or saw dust also adds nutrients back into the soil over time. This has been called the "Back to Eden" style. There is some debate as to using pine wood chips because they can alter the pH of the soil, but it doesn't seem to make a huge difference for growing. The other concern is that nitrogen is tied up by the mulch, but this is not a concern if you don't work the mulch into the soil.

DEALING WITH WEEDS BEFORE YOU PLANT

There are a number of ways to deal with weeds in an organic manner. Landscaping fabric or plastic sheeting will reduce the amount of weeds, though some find it ugly. You can cover it with mulch to make it more beautiful, but that will break down and you may have seedlings growing on top of your weed barrier. A thick layer of wood chip mulch will also help you to avoid most weed problems.

Fire is a cool way to take out young weed seedlings and to start with a clean slate in your garden.

Lucky for you, you have an expert at removing weeds, leaves, roots and all. Your kid or kids. I would say that between 3 and 8 would be the prime age, but removing weeds can be very therapeutic at any age. Get their little hands dirty. Just remind them to try to get all parts of the weeds. You can give them an implement to help, once again depending on age. Anything with sharp prongs has to be used gently and not swung around like a light saber, but little shovels work pretty well and you can show them stepping on the top to get it to dig in deeper. You can help by getting a broadfork, hoe, spade, or spading fork and loosening up the soil before the cleanup team comes in. Bigger kids can use those implements as well. Now, a word to the wise, the ability to differentiate between weeds and not weeds seems to escape some of the younger kids. Indiscriminate weeding works

great for them, but weeding between already established plants should be done with a watchful eye.

Borax, salt and vinegar, and hot water also work to kill weeds. Borax and salt/vinegar will kill anything, but these options should be saved for sidewalk cracks or other areas where you do not want to grow anything afterwards. These mixtures can also hurt your skin, so use gloves and do this one yourself.

The last and most awesome option is to use fire. Kill it with fire. Flame weeders are sold online and at the garden center. You attach a little tank of propane, spark, and, voila, fire. They come in a one flame variety and they come as a wide array of flame shooters that you can walk behind and kill a whole row of weeds. This works for little spring sprouts, but not huge plants, of course. You might start a forest fire! Some things with a large tap root might also survive. It is not recommended to till the weeds in as a weed prevention measure because the weeds will just pop and might do so with greater vigor because you did them the favor of distributing their roots everywhere.

DEALING WITH ROCKS

Once again, little kids love rocks, rock collecting, gathering rocks, so use them if you can to help reduce the number of rocks in the garden. You don't have to get rid off all the rocks, but you will know if you have a rocky garden that needs a little work.

Weed barriers work well to defend unused space from weeds like those pictured above.

N-P-K in Fertilizer

N - NITROGEN

P - PHOSPHOROUS

K - POTASSIUM

Based on current research a ratio of 3-1-2 or 6-2-4 works well for most garden plants. Most organic sources have a ratio of 1-1-1 or 2-2-2.

These should be combined with high nitrogen sources like urea or bloodmeal.

Organic fertilizers are easier to find at your local hardware store .

AMENDING YOUR SOIL

If you have performed a soil test, you will know the ratio of clay, to sand, to loam in your soil. If not, grab a scoop of your garden dirt and hold it in your hand. Is it sandy and brittle? It's mostly sandy. If you squeeze it does water come out? It's loamy. Does it stick together really well? It's mostly clay. If it is sandy or mostly clay, we want to incorporate more organic matter, like compost or a good balanced growing mix. You will also benefit from incorporating a nutrient-rich addition, like compost tea, fish meal, bone meal, or blood meal. You can use chicken manure or other manures, but they need to be composted to destroy harmful pathogens. These

Do not make a mulch volcano around the base of your trees ... so you do not rot the trunk with retained moisture.

organic fertilizers release nitrogen, phosphorous, and potassium (NPK) at a slow rate that will not burn or kill your seedlings. Different bagged organic fertilizers will have different ratios of listed NPK for different types of plants. Unless you are growing competition grade vegetables and herbs, you can get away with augmenting with a 1-1-1, 5-5-5 or something similar. Place the compost and fertilizer on top and then work it in a little bit with a hard-tined rake.

You can also use a tilther like the one to the left to integrate the amendments into the top of the soil layer.

ACCLIMATING SEEDLINGS

Before you transplant your seedlings outside, you are going to need to acclimate them to being outside. When we buy plants from the garden center we are used to just placing them in the garden and moving on. But when you buy them from the garden center they have been outside for a while. If you are growing seedlings yourself indoors, they are not used to bright outdoor sunlight. Place them outside for a few hours every day, increasing the outdoor time

over a few days. This will help them get used to being outside and save them from a shock that might kill them or hinder their growth.

PLANTING

To plant, make a hole the size of the pot or growing container and place the entire root system in the hole, with the bottom of the main stalk being even with the level of your garden. Some plants are sturdier than others. Go ahead and let your kids plant tomatoes, squash, peas, peppers, and most herbs and flowers. Push the plants out from the bottom. You can turn it on its side to help out. Do not pull the plant out by its stalk.

For direct sowing, make little furrows with your hand and toss the seeds into the middle of the trough. Then just scrap the mounds back into the furrow to bury the seeds. For very large plots, they sell seeders that will automatically furrow and place the seeds. Look up Jang Seeder for more information on this. You will have to buy different rollers for different sized seeds.

If you have not yet mulched, you are going to want to do so now. Just make sure to not get it on leaves or stems. Also, do not turn your trees and bushes into mulch volcanoes with mulch on the trunk. You want to make a little raised mound (doughnut-shaped) around the base of the trunk so you do not rot the trunk with retained moisture.

Option 2: Raised Beds and Containers

I am placing these two options together because container gardening is just using mini raised beds when you think about it. You also get the benefit of being able to move them around after they are filled, if they don't end up too heavy. A dolly will come in handy to move most filled pots.

Make sure that there are holes in the bottom of the container, covered with some broken ceramic pots or rocks, to help with drainage. Some people get really creative with what you can garden in, like using boots or old wheelbarrows, but this section will refer to your normal, garden-variety pots that are made specifically for growing plants.

Why might you want to use one of these containment options? If you are on a slope, have rocky or otherwise poor soil, have a groundhog or tunnelling rodent issue, or you have trouble bending down, you might want to try raised beds or container gardening. If you are on a slope, you will still have to level the area where you place your raised bed or containers, but you will not have to worry about soil erosion because it is held in the raised beds. If you have trouble bending down, then you will probably want the highest raised bed which will be about 32 inches for most commercially available kits. There are some large decorative pots which can also help with bending over, but the larger the container the more difficult it will be to move.

Containers can also be treated like mini-raised beds, and used where you have a concrete pad (such as a balcony or unused driveway) or they can be placed on soil. Using different heights of containers made of different materials allows you to add some artistic touches to your garden.

Raised beds in different stages of filling

MEASURE YOUR SPACE

You have probably already measured your space to help with garden planning, but raised beds pose some special placement requirements. They should be placed on level ground, so you will be levelling the area you are growing in. Large tree roots can be accommodated somewhat with cutting out the bottom of the raised beds, but it is not optimal. For slopes, this evening out of the soil will mean terracing, basically making dirt steps in the slope. Additionally, raised beds are rigid structures that should only be 4 to 4.5 feet wide if you want your kids to be able to reach to the middle for planting or harvesting. If you use a raised bed that is 6 ft. wide, they will not be able to reach small plants, but you can occupy the middle with a tree or bush. You may need a special implement or ladder to harvest from the tree.

Containers will be sourced more specifically to accommodate the type of plant you are growing, its current size, trellising needs, and its moisture requirements. To make a more cohesive collection, use fewer large pots planted with multiple varieties as opposed to many small pots with just one plant each.

SOURCE BUILDING MATERIALS AND/OR CONTAINERS AND POTS

Once you have measured out the space that you want to grow in using raised beds, then you will source the materials for building the raised bed. Kits are available in a variety of materials, from corrugated metal to cedar. Metal kits will include an internal strut system if you get one wider than 3 ft. These metal bars keep the two sides from bowing out when you put the soil in.

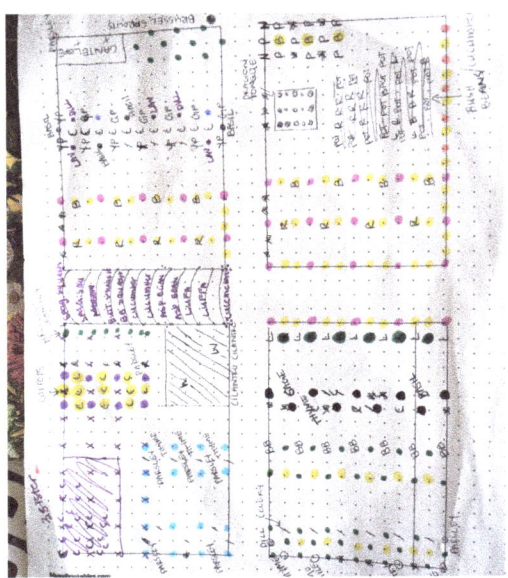

>> **Hand drawing on graph paper is easy. Just make each square represent 1/2 ft. or 1/4 ft. squared.**

Earthships have specialized growing cells that recycle grey water to provide nutrients and water to the plants

Raised beds come in a multitude of dimensions. Pick the ones that best suit your situation, but make sure to leave a buffer between each for walking.

Building and Placing Your Raised Beds

Remember to use an internal support system if you are building with bendy material like thin metal. Kits are great because they take care of all the details from design to execution, but they can be cost prohibitive.

If you want to build a simple raised bed, you can go to the local home improvement store and buy lumber and screws for your raised bed. Using several courses of 4 x 4 inch posts work because they are bulky and self supporting. You don't make a frame and then cover it with 2x4s. But that is also an option. You can also reuse pallets to build the frame.

When sourcing materials for an outdoor installation, there are a few things to think about. One, the inside and bottom of the bed will be touching dirt and water. This means you need something that will not rot (quickly) and will not leach dangerous chemicals into your soil.

This is especially important when using pallets. Only use heat-treated (marked with a HT) pallets, and not chemically-treated pallets to avoid introducing chemicals into your growing medium. All wood that touches the soil will eventually rot. Some woods are more rot resistant, like cedar, and there are things you can do to wood to help it resist moisture. For any lumber that is going into the ground, you can paint it with a waterproofing sealant or you can char it with a torch. Using metal posts would be better for longevity. If groundhogs or other tunnelling rodents are a concern in your area, you can cover the bottom with wire mesh to prohibit tunnelling.

Using organic plant matter to take up space in a raised bed is an excellent way to save money.

Ceramic pots, painted pots, metal troughs, plastic feed bins, and hanging pots are just a few of the many containers that you can use for growing. Ceramic pots are the most universal and come in a variety of sizes.

BUILD AND PLACE YOUR BEDS

Level the space, build your beds, and then move them to where they are going. You will want to leave at least 2 ft between them, but probably more like 3.5 feet because plants will get bushy and take over some of the space.

If you get a metal kit, you will be able to pick it up and move it. If you have a long wooden raised bed, you will want to build it in place. Remember your wire mesh on the bottom if you need to block rodents. If you need help to level out the area, you can place gravel under the raised bed. It is relatively easy to rake even, and it helps with drainage.

These beds were corrugated steel, coated in zinc, and painted with a USDA approved non-toxic paint. The kits come in 4-way kits, 6-way kits, and 10-way kits. This means that you have 4, 6, or 10 different ways you can configure them into different dimensions. These are 30 inch tall beds, two 4.5 by 8 ft and one 6 by 6 ft. The 8 ft long beds came with cross

struts to keep the walls from bowing out or in when they are filled with soil.

FILL YOUR BEDS AND CONTAINERS

You will fill the raised bed all the way. This is a kid-friendly activity!! We suggest filling ⅔ of the bed with wood rounds, branches, leaves and other organic material. This borrows from hugelkultur methods. For containers, the way that you fill them at this point will depend on if you are using seedlings or larger starts. You will not be filling the entire container if you are placing a dwarf citrus tree in it, for example. For smaller pots, the ratio of organic matter to soil will be different. You want a good deal of soil, at least 6 inches, so you may only have a few inches of wood chips on the bottom. You can also use perlite in addition to branches, leaves, and wood chips to lighten up a large pot and fill extra space if you have a very tall pot. The organic material will fill the space cheaply and will decay over time to make soil in the long run. It also helps to retain moisture.

So gather the kids and have them help you out with this one. In the raised beds, we had our son place the branches evenly over the wood rounds. The rounds will be pretty heavy, so have an adult place those first and then let the kids do the rest. The last ⅓ will be soil, compost, fertilizer, and a nice layer

of mulch on the top. You want at least 6 inches of soil. You might have to top off the raised bed every year because the rotting wood breaks down. But you will want to renew the beds every year anyway.

PLANT YOUR PLANTS!

Follow your grid plan and place your plants accordingly. When plants start growing like crazy, you will have to rein them in or keep them trim. Climbing plants will need a trellis. Sugar snap peas, snow peas, beans, and nasturtium will grow up nearly anything. For determinate tomatoes and peppers, using a cage will help keep them from bushing out over everything else.

Summer squashes, winter squashes, watermelons, and other vining fruits and vegetables can hang over the edge and keep growing if you have room. Just remember that you are the boss! You don't have to let it keep growing all willy nilly. You can grow them over a trellis between the beds or up a close fence. Or you can trim them and help the fruits that you have get the most nutrients so they can grow large and robust.

After you have planted, it's time for maintenance. Your family's work is not over. Let's talk about the next steps before harvesting, but first we have one more option, hugelkultur!

Just remember that you are the boss!

You don't have to let it keep growing all willy nilly.

Filling your beds with organic garden waste, tree limbs, and leaves saves a lot of money

A wooden frame lined with corrugated metal is a wonderful option for a raised bed.

Flame treat the wood to help with longevity.

Option 3: Hugelkultur Beds

GATHERING ORGANIC MATTER

Turn that fallen tree into dirt with hugelkultur. This will require a chainsaw or you can get already sawn rounds. You want to use trees that degrade relatively quickly. Do not use Cedar, Black locust, Black cherry, or Black walnut because they take a longer time to break down and/or have growth inhibiting properties. Take a pruner or a small hand saw to the branches. Gather leaves and straw. After you have gathered materials, you will start assembling them in layers.

ASSEMBLING THE MOUND

Pick the orientation that works best for your landscape. Depending on the orientation, you might create microclimates. With an East-West orientation, your northerly side will be slightly cooler. With a North-South orientation, both sides will be more equal in terms of sunlight. Starting with a trench ranging from 1 to 3 ft deep, you fill in the center of the hugelkultur mound with wood rounds or large branches. Large branches are covered with smaller branches, wood chips. Kids make excellent structural engineers when it comes to placing dead plant material into a mound shape.

Ideally, it has a few weeks to settle before you plant into it. The decaying wood, straw, leaves, and additional organic material help to retain moisture, making it ideal for dealing with drought in drier regions. The decaying wood over time also turns into a rich soil. Some plants love this as it mimics their natural growing environment. Strawberries, yarrow, mint, borage, and squash would do very well in a hugelkultur mound.

Turn garden wast[e] into hugelkultur beds as a cost-effective way to make fertile soil that does not contain rocks.

Anything with a deep taproot will have difficulty growing into a large specimen. Other plants like asparagus, do not like to compete with other plants or weeds, so they would do better in a dedicated space.

Once again, here are the layers in different stages of progress as we implemented them in the raised beds in our geodesic greenhouse. The outer slope for a real outdoor hugelkultur mound should end up around 45 degrees.

If you find that erosion is a problem while you are waiting for the hugelkultur mound to settle, you can start some cover crops like vetch, fava beans, or crimson clover, which will act as nitrogen-fixers. Plant your seedlings or starts accordingly.

Borage will also self-seed and take over a bed.

PLANTING

Hugelkultur is perfect for permaculture guilds where each plant helps and supports the other plants in the guild. Berry bushes as a middle layer would do well as a main plant to anchor your planting. Strawberries or other crawling plants like thyme can fill out the last layer. You can interplant lettuce or any number of herbs to fill in the rest of the space.

One thing to be careful of are those plants that can be invasive and overtake the rest of the plants. In a way, all interplanting becomes a fight of the fittest, but you want to keep the cheaters out of the fight and this includes invasive self-seeders and plants with running rhizomes or roots.

Mint is notorious for taking over and the nature of a hugelkultur mound would mean that it would be even more difficult to remove mint and all of its roots.

Hugelkultur mound ready for planting

Trellising, weed fabric, and organic pest control will line you up for success

06

Garden Maintenance: Watering Fertilizing & Weeding Pest Control

>>

The best weed control is prevention

>>

Caterpillars and hornworms can take out large sections of plants very quickly

A gentle watering
wand should spray
a light rain-like jet

These sprayers are
not your friend.
Leave them for
shooing away
animals.

Watering

Let's start with watering because this is one of those easy fixes if you think you don't have a green thumb. It is key that you have prepared your soil well and that you have a layer of mulch placed to help retain moisture.

Key item number two: You have to soak your plants' roots! Watering the leaves, the tree bark, and the flowers is not watering your plant. Tell the kids! Get a soaker wand sprayer and hand water everything. This is super fun for kids, and perfect for hot summer days. Give each plant 30-60 seconds of attention with the hand-held soaker sprayer. Your goal is to soak down to 6 inches below the surface of your soil to make sure that the roots get water. Aim for watering at least twice a week, unless you live somewhere that gets a rainforest level of precipitation. You may need to water more often during a heatwave.

Containers are a slightly different story. There is generally less organic matter to retain moisture and they also tend to lose moisture through evaporation from the container more quickly than in-ground or hugelkultur growing, so you will want to water containers once a day.

If you simply do not have the time or patience, then set up an overhead broadcasting sprinkler, like a Rainbird. Kids also love playing in the sprinkler of course. This will be less efficient and some plants don't really like their leaves getting wet because of mildew issues, but sprinklers are better than nothing. You can also try using drip tape. Drip tape runs along to base of the plants and drips for a given period of time.

Set the timer for early in the morning or later in the day to help the water soak in before or after the heat of the day. You want enough water on your garden that you see it puddling. This lets you know that you have reached a certain level of saturation. Drip tape is a more efficient option, but laying it out and staking it in place is more time consuming and costly.

Fertilizing and Composting

This seems to be the most mysterious aspect of growing for most people, adults and kids alike. Most people wonder why we even need to fertilize. I mean, does nature fertilize? Well, yes, but it doesn't seem like it. And things still grow.

We have already covered some of the basics of amending your soil, including the definition of N-P-K and what ratio you want for most garden plants (see pg. 54).

For ongoing treatment, we have a few additional options that go beyond your initial amending of the soil. You will want to fertilize every few weeks with these methods.

FISH EMULSION

Hydrolyzed fish constitutes the main ingredient for many commercially available organic plant foods. Fish emulsion can be diluted with water and sprayed onto crops. Some plants like this method of fertilization because it gets absorbed through the leaves. This is called foliar action and if it is delivered through a drip feed or overhead system it is called fertigation.

COMPOST TEA

Compost tea or comfrey leaf tea can also be used to fertilize plants in an organic manner. Compost tea is something that you can make if you have a compost bin. You basically get the "drippings" and use those. Comfrey tea can be made easily by soaking comfrey leaves for 20 days and then watering your plants with that solution.

There are quite a few plant specific organic brands that you can use for tomatoes, roses, azaleas, or general vegetable growth. Most of these are granules that you apply directly to the soil, away from the main stalk of the plant.

You will want to add fertilizer into the hole when you first plant a seedling, if you have larger starts. The next application of fertilizer will depend on what kind you are using. Fish emulsion fertilizer can be sprayed onto crops every other week. Some pelleted fertilizer will be applied once a month. My bag of tomato food says to feed your tomatoes 14 days after planting with 3 tablespoons placed around the stalk of the plant and watered in.

"CHOP AND DROP" MULCH

You can use some plants to "chop and drop" as a living mulch that will provide nutrients as it decays over time. Banana leaves and comfrey are two plants that provide plenty of extra materials that can be used to mulch an area in an organic manner. This works well for larger plants, like apple trees, because they block weeds as well as providing nutrition.

> **Composting turn trash into treasure. Make sure to combine equal parts of "brown" and "green" waste for a carbon and nitrogen-rich mix.**

This is my compost. You want equal parts green and brown matter.

COMPOST AND COMPOSTING

Now is also the time to start your compost pile if you don't have one already. You will be taking your garden waste, kitchen waste, dead leaves, grass, coffee grounds, eggs, and rotten fruit and throwing it into a big pile.

Ideally, you have a three pile system where you are moving piles over as they decompose so you can stir them up and moisten them. Keep your pile moist and it will become hot as bacteria work to break down the material to make compost.

COMPOST RECIPE

Equal parts brown (carbon-rich) and green (nitrogen-rich) inputs

Brown = dead leaves, wood chips, shredded paper, straw, cardboard (remove labels), sawdust, hay

Green = fruit/vegetable scraps, eggs, coffee grounds, grass and plant clippings

The lovely but spiky thistle is a hand stabber. Use gloves and a weeding tool to remove

Some weeds, like this purple dead nettle, can be used as medicine, so you might want to use them instead of tossing them in the compost bin

Weeding can be fun!

v
v

What is a weed exactly? It's any plant that you don't want there. It's as simple as that. With small weed seedlings, there are few distinguishing characteristics apart from being where they are not supposed to be.

The answer to weeds is prevention. Tarping for a few months before you plant will sprout weeds and then kill them. Landscaping fabric and/or thick layers of mulch will keep most weeds at bay. Flameweeding before you plant will also help to reset your system by killing the surface seeds and seedlings. But let's say you still have a few weeds popping up...

After the initial preparation of your growing area you will need to weed as often as possible to keep up with your plants. Smaller weeds are easier to take out than larger weeds! There are a few fun tools you can use for this depending on the size of the weed.

For little seedlings, using a hoe works well. All you have to do is rake the weed roots out of the ground. You can even leave them on the surface to die and turn to mulch. Larger weeds will require a garden fork or trowel, and your hands will almost always work.

WEED IDENTIFICATION

What is a weed? To be honest, a weed is just a plant you don't want there. A rose bush in your lettuce patch is a weed if it's not supposed to be there.

The first step is to identify what is not a weed in your garden. As you are growing your seeds and when you plant them, take notice of how they look and have your kids point out some of the identifying features. What do the leaves look like? Do they have tendrils, like a pea plant, that help them climb?

You can even have them draw what the leaves look like and identify other parts of the plant as part of a Kids' Garden Journal. This will help to cement the plant parts

into their memory forever.

Now we can identify what is a weed. Weeds are considered invasive plants that out-compete what you would like to grow. They are born and bred to win the ecosystem game.

Dandelions, nettles, cleavers, grasses and spurge are common weeds all over the United States. Most of these can be pulled with your hands, though stinging nettles and puncturevine will require tough gloves and a trowel to remove. For all weeds, you will want to make sure that you get the entire root system.

DEEP TAPROOTS

For some weeds with deep tap roots you need to loosen the soil around it with a shovel, spade, or gardening fork. Some plants that are

FUN PROJECT ALERT!

Have your kids identify common weeds as part of their Kid's Journal. Drawing the eaves and flowers will help them to remember.

You can use a plant ID app to help identify them or you can crowd source the identification by asking an online forum.

really difficult to control, like Japanese Knotweed, can be treated with harsher measures including boiling water or vinegar and salt.

Creeping buttercup, purple dead nettle, wild green garlic, crabgrass are all over this Tennessee property. Feel free to pull them all out if they are growing in your gardening space. Purple dead nettle and wild green garlic can be eaten and used in a medicinal way as well. The common weed broadleaf plantain also works to ease insect bite pain. You chew it up and place it on the bite as a poultice, so it's a good idea to keep some of this around in case you get bit while working out in the garden.

Plantain makes a great poultice to treat bug bites and strings

THE RIGHT TOOLS

Every year a new gardening gadget comes out that guarantees to make you life easier, but most garden tools that work really well have been around for millennia. These staples are something you should get and teach your kids about.

Hoes, garden forks, and long-handled cultivators can ease your weeding trials by making it so you don't have to bend over. Hoes pull out seedlings from the tops of the soil by loosening the top layer and disconnecting the roots, as it were. Part of your regular maintanence will be hoeing for small weeds between your plants once a week. Getting these little sprouts before they go to seed is an important step in weed prevention.

Garden forks are used to get under larger weeds,

Weeds, cleavers, in our dragon fruit containers

Hoes are a simple way to deal with weeds, but you have to do it every week. Here we have a double-sided hoe/fork, a stirrup hoe. and a regular hoe.

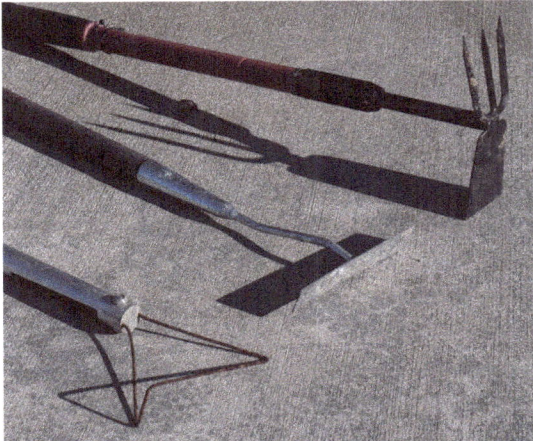

A wire hoe for loose soil with small seedlings, a bar hoe for scraping, and a double-sided how with adjustable handle for up-close work or extended hoeing.

Wild mustard is a common weed in the Southeastern US.

one's whose roots are more well established. Long-handled cultivators have claw-like tines that really dig and can get out most weeds. With any of these purely mechanical solutions, you need to get the roots of the weeds out of the soil. Ideally, this occurs before they get out of hand.

Some invasive plants, like crabgrass, bamboo and mint, have runners that travel feet under the ground and pop up on the other sides of fences and borders. Getting out all the roots is one half of the equation. The other half to dealing with them is either only growing them in containers or running their growing barriers deeper into the ground to prevent their spread.

ORGANIC ALTERNATIVES TO CHEMICALS

Traditional weed killers are also general plant killers and human biome killers. Organic alternatives include a vinegar, soap, and salt solution, hot water, and flame weeding. A list of your alternatives is included on the right.

Start with the basics in terms of tools before splurging on one-use items.

A regular garden hoe, a good spade, and a hand cultivator are a great start to a solid gardening tool collection. After a few seasons, you can buy, rent, or borrow other tools to test them out and see how you like them.

Organic Weed Killer Recipes

SALT, VINEGAR, AND SOAP RECIPE

- 1 cup Epsom Salt
- 1/2 gallon vinegar
- 1/8 cup dish soap

Simply mix all of these ingredients together and pour into a sprayer. Apply to any areas where you want to kill all of the plants. This washes away in the rain, so you will reapply when you want to kill weeds again.

CITRUS OIL AND DISH SOAP

- 1 gallon vinegar
- 2 ounces dish soap
- 1 tablespoon citrus oil

Once again, mix everything together, place into spray bottle, and spray all parts of the weed, including the undersides of the leaves and the base of the plant. This may require a few applications to work.

BOILING WATER

- 1 pot boiling water

Just what it says. Pour boiling hot water onto weeds and you will kill them. Just make sure that you don't use this to kill weeds whose roots are close to the plants the you want to keep.

Bees are your
friends in the
garden

Before we talk about pest control:
A Save the Bees PSA

This Public Service Announcement is brought to you by the "Every living thing on this planet relies on bees" gardening group. Feel free to support us by planting more flowering plants or letting some of your crops go to seed.

Bees. We have to love the bees. Their numbers are collapsing all over the globe for various reasons, but we have the power to help them.

GO ORGANIC PLUS

Organic is a good place to start because you are eschewing the use of broad-spectrum poisons. Any pesticide that kills most bugs will also kill bees (acute pesticide poisoning) or at least weaken their immune system so that they succumb to Varroa mites, Israeli Acute Paralysis virus, and the gut parasite Nosema far more easily. So not using pesticides on crops or your garden is a good start, but we also have to provide them with flowers to pollinate and gather nectar from and we have to make sure that our organic methods are not hurting or impeding them.

PLANTING POLLINATOR FRIENDLY PLANTS

Bees need flowers. Flowers need bees. Some say that they have a "relationship." So that means that increasing the number of flowers on your property will help them immensely. You can do this in a few ways. One, you can plant pollinator friendly plants like borage, calendula, bee balm (monarda), butterfly milkweed, black-eyed susans, pasture rose, purple passionflower (Passiflora incarnata), and New York ironweed.

A few of these are also edible for you and your littles, like borage and calendula. When you harvest them, leave some of the flowers for the bees. Some are also medicinal. Once again, plant them and leave some for the bees.

Your second option is to let some of your garden plant "go to seed." First, some vegetables will flower and then they will form seeds. "Going to seed" is the term that is used for certain plants when they go past the vegetative stage in the flowering stage. Brassicas, like broccoli and cabbage, basil, lettuces, arugula, and carrots will bolt or flower after they are done with their season.

For most vegetables, this signifies that they are now bitter (basil and arugula) or have turned woody (carrots and turnips). Basically, they are done and you don't want to eat them. You can pull these plants and throw them into your compost or you can let them flower to feed the bees. This is especially important if their are few other options in your garden as occurs during the fall season. The bonus to letting them flower is that you can save seeds from these plants.

DO NOT TREAT OR COVER PLANTS WHEN THEY ARE FLOWERING

Certain organic pest control methods conflict with bee happiness. One is covering your plants with netting while they are flowering. The bees can't get to those tasty flowers and pollinate them. You will not have tomatoes, peppers, golden berries, watermelons, cantaloupes, or eggplant without pollinators.

Do not use diatomaceous earth when your plant is flowering because it will also hurt or kill bees. Neem oil is also not recommended even though it is considered safe for bees. Only treat with neem at dusk or dawn because bees forage during midday runs.

This arugula and spinach are flowering in the greenhouse because of the warm temperatures.

Organic Pest Control

You can plant a "pest trap" or sacrificial part of your garden to help mitigate some of the ravages of common garden insects. (pg. 24). You may find that you unintentionally have a "sacrificial" plant that all the aphids and white flies just love. If you do, consider leaving it in there for them to feast on if it means leaving the rest of your plants alone. But maybe you have one or two or three thousand aphids on some other plants that you want to deter or ... destroy. We got you covered.

PEST SPECIFIC CONTROLS

Organic pest controls are not one size fits all. Some of them are for flying pests, some are for crawling pests. Some rely on smell, some are mechanical, for lack of a better descriptor. Some are straight-up biological warfare. All is fair in love and organic pest control.

DIATOMACEOUS EARTH (DE)

This one is specifically for crawling insects (slugs, beetles, worms, fleas, mites, and spiders) and the way it works is mechanical. Diatomaceous earth is ground up diatoms, which are sea creatures with little exoskeletons-shells. This fine powder gets into the chitin and outer armor of beetles, ants, and other creepy crawlers.

Add diatomaceous earth to water to form a sprayable solution and spray it over your plants. You can also take a spoon and distribute it over an area that they crawl or walk through. The powder gets stuck in their joints and kills them. That's it. Anything bigger, without bug armor, is fine. Just don't get it in your eyes or soft tender tissues because it can be irritating.

Pleas note that this method will also inhibit and possibly kill pollinators. So use DE only when you don't have flowers that need to be pollinated.

Diatomaceous earth is one of the most effective methods for treating pests and a safe option for children and adults.

NEEM OIL AND SOAP

This is more for your soft bodied and flying insects, like aphids and white flies. Neem oil is a multi-faceted approach to pest control. When you douse aphids with them it will kill them, but it 's smell also acts as a deterrent. The main active component of neem oil is Azadirachtin. This component reduces insect feeding and interferes with insect hormone balance.

Do not spray it in your eyes and wash your hands after applying, as it can be irritating to eyes and skin. It does not cause cancer. In fact, some studies have shown that it slows the growth of certain cancers.

It does break down quickly so only mix up as much as you need for a single application. The recipe is on the next page. The soap acts as an emulsifier to help the oil and water mix and stay mixed.

Organic Pest Control Recipes

DIATOMACEOUS EARTH MIX

· 1 cup Diatomaceous earth
· (optional) 1/2 gallon water

You can use DE all by itself by dusting it where the pests are, or in there path (obvious with slugs). You can also mix it with water and spray it onto plants which works better for treating the undersides of leaves.

NEEM OIL AND SOAP

· 1 gallon water
· 2 teaspoons dish soap
· 1-2 tablespoons neem oil

Begin with mixing soap and water. Then add the neem oil. Place into spray bottle, and spray all parts of the plant, including the undersides of the leaves and the base of the plant. This will take some time as this mix effects the eating behavior and reproduction of the pests, reducing numbers over time.

Diatomaceous earth is a kid-friendly way to take care of your pests.

Btk

Bacilllus thuringiensis kurtsaki (Btk) is an excellent organic option for dealing with most leaf-eating caterpillars, including tomato hornworms, gypsy moth larvae, cabbage looper, and cabbage worms. It is a bacteria that specifically attacks these species, specifically their gut. After ingestion, their gut explodes and they die. To find an organic Btk, look for an OMRI certified label on the bottle.

MANUAL PEST CONTROL

You can also pick the tomato hornworm off the tomato (or other nightshade) plant and step on them, which is very satisfying.

Pro tip: They glow under blacklight! Get a blacklight and go on a night hunt for a fun pest-tromping time.

If you have chickens, the tomato has a toxin in it called solanine, which will be transmitted to them if you feed them hornworms that have been feeding on tomato.

You can also place rubbing alcohol on a cotton swab and manually scrap off aphids in the garden. This works well on smaller plants where you can reach all parts.

Japanese beetles can also be knocked into a bucket of soapy water. Just do it early in the morning before they wake up fully and swarm.

Caterpillar tunnels stretched over with bug netting and weighed down by sand bags

Bug netting on the side of a greenhouse to allow cross ventilation.

COVERING YOUR PLANTS

Caterpillar tunnels or row covers can be used to just keep pests away from your plants. Bug netting, basically, just blocks them from getting to your plants in the first place.

Netting needs to be stretched tight over a frame and secured with weights or sand bags to keep it as bug proof as possible.

The plants can either be watered overhead or by drip tape. The netting is also permeable to rain and allows for ventilation. Netting will also keep birds out that might try to eat newly seeded areas. Remove the netting to allow pollinators to get to your plants when they are flowering so that they will produce fruit.

PREDATORY BUGS

Perhaps the most enlightening, scientific, and downright cool way to get rid of malicious bugs is with predatory bugs. These are bugs that don't eat your plants, but they will eat your pests. The classic example is ladybugs that eat your aphids. Praying mantises will also eat pretty much anything, but be careful because they will also eat your beneficial insects, like bees and butterflies.

Green lacewings can be the most versatile because they are larger than ladybugs and will not attact beneficial insects. The larvae are quite ravenous and will eat up to 200 insects a week.

You can purchase green lacewing larvae or eggs, ladybugs, or praying mantises online. Sometimes they are also available at your local garden center in a

Predatory Bug	Prey Pests
Ladybugs	aphids, thrips, tiny caterpillars, mites, leafhoppers, and scale insects
Praying Mantises (warning: also eats bees and butterflies)	locusts, spiders, caterpillars, beetles, adult moths, wasps, and aphids
Green Lacewings (larvae)	spider mites, caterpillars, thrips, whiteflies, aphids, mealybugs, and leafhoppers
Spiders (warning: will also eat beneficial bugs)	caterpillars, fruit flies, aphids, wasps, and grasshoppers
Hoverflies (larvae)	aphids, beetles, caterpillars, thrips, mealybugs, and scale insects

refrigerated case.

Each of these predatory insects have specific instructions for their release. So, make sure that you read them and understand how to release them and when to release them. For example, ladybugs need to be released during the cooler part of your day in the early evening.

You can open the container under a box outside which you leave out overnight. Make sure to lightly spray the surrounding plants so they have some moisture to intake when they start roaming around when the day heats up.

Green lacewing larvae should be released immediately upon getting them because they can start to eat each other. Eggs will turn grey when they are about the hatch.

Spider on the underside of an aloe plant

Fake Ladybug! This is an Asian lady beetle. See the black "M' marking on the back of its head

07

Harvesting, Preserving, and Storing

Growing your own fruits, vegetables, and herbs will guarantee a greater level of confidence and ability for you and your children.

>> Hey family! You've worked hard this growing season and it's time to collect the fruits (and vegetables) of your labor. Time for preservation and storage.

There is life after the harvest! Let's take stock and think about the future.

Giving the gift of a green thumb will set the future generations up for success no matter where they live.

Fresh radishes
from the garden
with their greens
cut off

**Work smarter, not harder.
Use the right tool for harvesting
to mitigate ripping and bruising.**

A garden fork works well to
loosen up the soil around root >>
vegetables. Just make sure
not to start to close to the
roots or you may chop it in
half accidentally.

From seedlings to full grown heads of curly lettuce

Harvest Time

Get a basket, an apron with pockets, or a garden cart first. Now for the tools. Let's go through each type of plant type by type and see what we do when we harvest. First of all, for any of these plants we want to make sure that we have the right tool, the right approach, and the right timing.

HERBS

Your friend here will be your local, friendly kitchen scissors or shears. For most herbs, the correct time to harvest is going to be anytime before they "bolt" or go to flower. Annual plants like basil, cilantro, and parsley bolt when the weather gets warm. Basil and cilantro will become more bitter and tougher. Parsley will be fine.

BOLTING

Here are a few ways to keep your herbs (and some vegetables) from bolting.

1) Mulch well. This will insulate the roots somewhat and keep them cooler.
2) Harvest from your herbs frequently. This helps in two ways. It will promote more growth in plants like basil because new growth will stem off in two branches. You will also be trimming off potential flowering buds.
3) Cut off flowers when they do appear to prolong your season. This does not work for cilantro or salad greens like arugula. Once they start to bolt, let them go to seed and save for next season.
4) Try to promote vegetative growth with a high-nitrogen and low phosphorous blend because phosphorous triggers flower development while nitrogen promotes leaf growth.

ROOT VEGETABLES

Carrots, radishes, and turnips will be pulled when they are ready. Depending on the variety, carrots will range from 3-7 inches. Radishes should be quarter to half-dollar size. Turnips will range from golf ball to tennis ball size.

We may be tempted to leave them in longer to get bigger. One thing though: bigger is not better when it comes to root vegetables. After their optimal size, they become mealy and inedible. And they are closer to bolting.

Harvest by pulling them out with your hands. If the soil is particularly clay-ey or hard, water first to loosen up or use a garden fork to leverage them out.

BOLTING

Root vegetables can also bolt, especially if they get too much heat, too little water, or too much stress. Poor soil will also stress a plant.

Either pick the plant right away if you see little flower buds and see if it is still edible or let it go to seed to collect for next year. Cutting off the flower stems will not reset root vegetables. Leaving them to flower will also provide flowers for the pollinators.

Harvest your plants when they are ready! Usually this means right before they go bad. Some plants will be picked by size and some will be picked by color.

NIGHTSHADES

Tomatoes and peppers have the benefit of coloring to let you know when they are ready. Red or orange varieties (or Black Krim or Purple Cherokee) will be that color when you pick them. If you pick them early or they haven't turned before the end of the growing season, there are methods that you can use to help them mature or you can prepare them when they are still green. I'll share those recipes with you in the preserving section.

In the meantime, you will be using a little pair of clippers to harvest peppers and tomatoes. Tomatoes can also be popped off the vine and eaten fresh from the garden (because they are organic and don't have pesticides covering them).

Eggplants harvesting will be more about size. They start off purple or white or purple with white stripes and just get bigger. Pick them at the size you want to enjoy them at. Smaller means more tender and less bitter. If they get too large and you still want to cook with them, soak them in salt water beforehand.

Use clippers and wear gloves when harvesting eggplants because they have little spikes on the top leaves and they can be quite painful if you grab bare-handed. Also, they have a stringy center to the stem which makes them impossible to just twist off.

POTATOES

Potatoes are nightshades, but you may have noticed that they don't grow like tomatoes, peppers, or eggplants. Sweet potatoes are not nightshades, by the way.

Harvest potatoes when the tops of the vines have died. Harvesting methods depend on whether you are collecting for dinner or for long term storage. Use a shovel, garden fork, or spading fork to carefully lift the plant out of the soil and just take the potatoes you need, if you are collecting for tonight's dinner. Water the leftovers back in to help the soil settle.

For long-term storage, you want to wait until the skins are thick and mature. The skin will not rub off easily. If that is the case, leave them in the soil for a longer period of time and then harvest and store in a cool, dry location.

SALAD GREENS

Lettuce, baby kale, arugula, tatsoi, and mizuna are all salad mix favorites in our household. For individual leaves you will use a pair of kitchen scissors. There is a tool called the "Quick Greens Harvester" which makes this process quicker for commercial operations, but scissors works for the average home.

For head lettuce, you will use a sharp knife. This will be a grownup activity or teenager with gloves activity. Some lettuces are also cut and come again, so you want to make sure that you leave enough stem for it to grow back. The Salanova varieties work like this and you can get as many a 4 cuts from these.

No, not these scissors

Kitchen shears work well for individual leaves

Cherry tomatoes on the vine ripen in vibrant rainbow from red or orange to green

> ❝
> # The thankful receiver bears a plentiful harvest.
>
> ### William Blake

Purple potato vines growing in a raised bed

FUN PROJECT ALERT!

Remember to get pictures or drawings of your harvest in your journals.

And the results of your taste tests!

Would you grow this again next year?

Which was your most favorite? Is it a new thing, or is it an old favorite?

Zucchini squash flowers are edible. You can batter them and fry them.

SUMMER SQUASHES

Yellow and green zucchini, pattypan squash, and chayote squash grow on vines that can get really long. By the end of the summer, you might be way over how many squash you are harvesting. To harvest, you will use a field knife that you pull from under the stem about one to two inches from where it meets the vine.

WINTER SQUASHES

Winter squash will be harvested in a similar manner as summer squashes, but the stems will be tougher. Pumpkins, butternut squash, acorn squash, kabocha squash, and any other hard-skinned storage squash or gourd are ready to harvest when the leaves and vines have died back. This will be in the fall for most varieties.

A sharp knife will be your friend and your enemy, but it has to be sharp to harvest quickly and efficiently.

Winter squashes are great for long-term storage, so you don't have to worry about growing too many of them. The only caveat is that they do take up a lot of room in your garden. Any extra can be displayed for the fall holidays or even given away as gifts. Some, like the birdhouse gourd, can be used for decoration or for the birds.

GARLIC

Garlic is easy to harvest if you know when. When the tips of the leaves turn brown, it is time to harvest. Use a spade or trowel to loosen the ground around the garlic. This step is necessary because otherwise you will just be breaking the leaves off. Grab the stem down by the ground and pull gently.

When your hardneck variety of garlic sprouts scapes earlier in the season, these can also be harvested and eaten which actually helps the bulb get bigger and more nutritious. Just cut the scape off below the big curve and sauté.

Garlic needs to be cured before it can be eaten. Lay it out to dry in one layer on a table that gets ventilation and then you can store it for the entire winter if need be.

Kabocha squash is often used in Thai Pumpkin Soup. You can eat the thin skin and this makes it an easier crop to process.

Green onions can be chopped and dried or freeze-dried for long term storage

Preserving the Harvest

Look, I don't want to leave you hanging with your harvest out and no plans for the future. This isn't something that is covered in most gardening books, but there is life after harvest.

Assuming you have been eating out of your garden regularly, there will come a time at the end of the season where you have an abundance of produce that you simply do not have time to cook before it spoils. This section is for that time.

A lot of these methods can use kitchen helpers to wash, chop, and prepare herbs and vegetables for preservation.

> **Fire is a cool way to take out young weed seedlings and to start with a clean slate in your garden.**

FREEZING

This is by far the easiest way to deal with most of your excess produce. However, this will take up freezer space pretty quickly. Sweet peppers, corn, onions, and tomatoes can be frozen without blanching. Okra, asparagus, leafy greens, and string beans must be blanched before freezing.

Blanching, placing in boiling water, stops the enzymatic activity that causes these vegetables to decay. Some vegetables don't do well with freezing, like lettuce and potatoes. Let the lettuce bolt for seeds and preserve the potatoes in another way.

This preservation time is another great thing to note in your journal and thinking on this will help you to tweak how much of this crop will you want to grow next year. Maybe you only need two squash plants instead of six.

DEHYDRATING

You can dehydrate a surprising amount of vegetables, fruits, flowers, and herbs. You can use your oven set to its lowest setting with the door propped open or you can purchase a dehydrator at different price levels. Take care to dry only similar items at the same time because different crops, parts of the plant, and thicknesses of cuts take different times and temperatures to dry.

Sundried tomatoes, dehydrated onion, dried basil and garlic powder are all things that you can make from your summer harvest. You can place these all in a coffee grinder and have a wonderful Italian-inspired spice mix.

You can also dry zucchini and some other starchy vegetables to grind into a soup mix thickener filled with nutrients and vitamins. This is a good way to add vegetables into your kids' food if they are perhaps still not into vegetables. Adding to pizza sauce, for example, works pretty well for adding broccoli to a fun easily consumed food.

CANNING

Canning seems to be daunting to

a lot of people because of the heat and pressure aspect of it. However, there are all types of canning and some are just easier and less scary.

The easiest is the quick pickle method. This is not a solution for long-term storage, but it will extend your eating window for items like radishes. In the refrigerator, quick pickles will last for two weeks.

For longer term storage, you do need a certain acidity and to boil the mason jars filled with your goodies. You just need a large stock pot, tongs, jars, lids, and to keep everything sanitary. You can make dill pickles, pickled okra, or pickled green tomatoes this way and they will store for months.

Radish Quick-le Pickle Recipe

Ingredients:

· 2 cups sliced radishes
· 1 tsp. peppercorn
· 1/2 tsp. chilli powder or dried cayenne peppers
· 1 cup white vinegar
· 1 cup water
· 1 tsp. Kosher salt
· 1 tbsp. brown sugar

Place the radish slices, peppercorn, and chilli peppers in a sterilized pint jar. Pack it in. Bring the other ingredients to a gentle boil to dissolve the salt and sugar. Pour over the radishes, etc. Cover and refrigerate for up to 2 weeks.

Dehydrating and canning are two ways to preserve for use during the winter

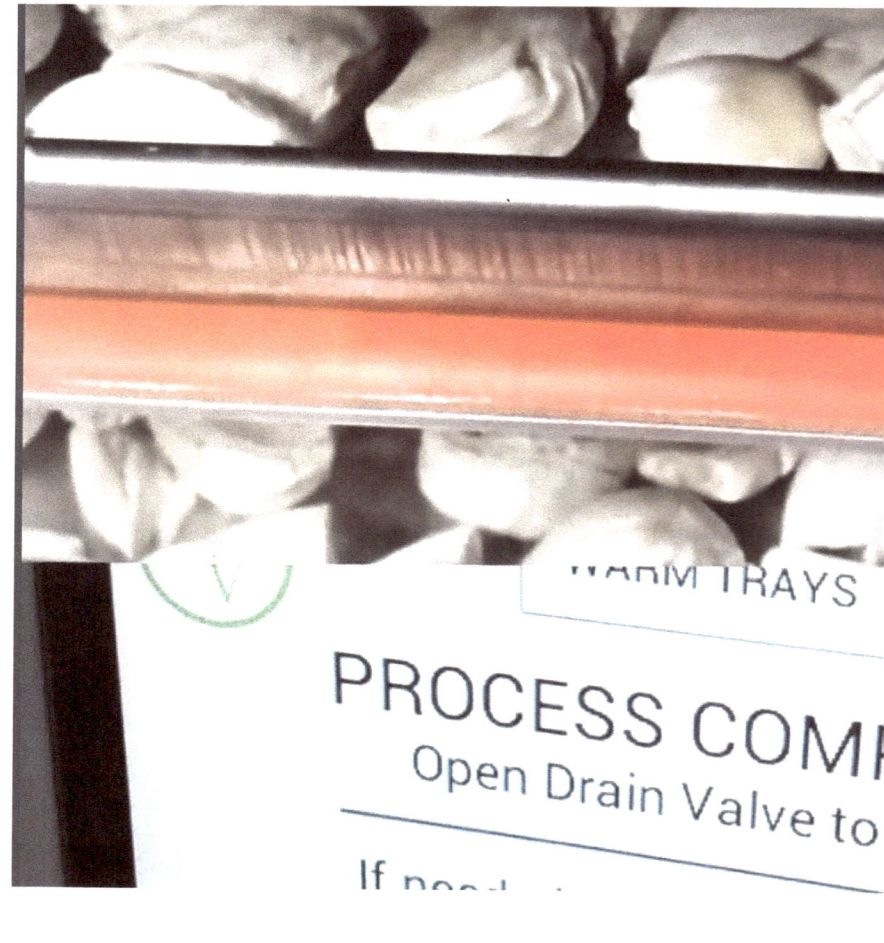

Fun (Optional) Kitchen Tools

Mandolin with hand guard: Makes slicing consistently thin slices of any vegetable possible

Dehydrator: Takes the guesswork out of temperature regulation and ventilation with labelled thermostat and built-in fan

Freeze Dryer: Literally anything can be freeze-dried, not just fruits and vegetables but eggs and lasagna. Ice cream!

Mortar and pestle: A must have for grinding spices or garlic to add to pickle solutions.

Canning equipment: Mason jars, lids, a stock pot for boiling are good starters. A pressure canner is needed for low-acidity items.

For low acid foods, pressure canning is the only way, but we won't be covering that because it is a hefty topic that needs its own book.

FERMENTING

This is also a whole book type of topic. But I just want to let you know that it is an option. This is especially the best option for cabbage based sauerkraut or kimchi.

Hot sauce made with a hot Thai pepper mash, fermented salsa, and fruit-based meads are ways in which our ancient cultures have not only preserved food, but have increased their bioavailability. These cultured foods also support a healthy immune system by bolstering the beneficial

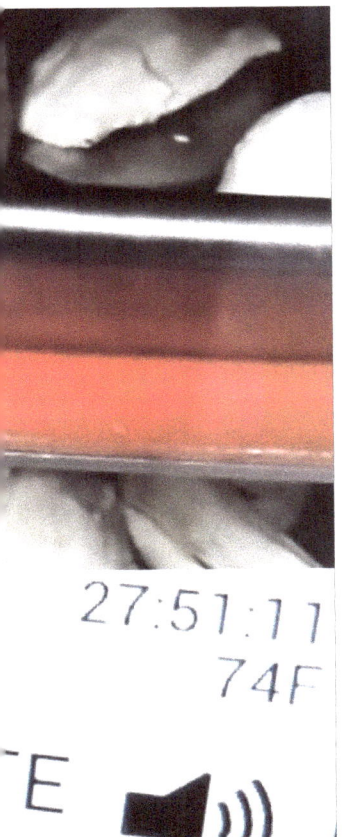

27:51:11
74F

Take into account what you like. Not everyone likes pickles, but then again maybe they like pickled okra and have just never tried it.

bacteria in your gut biome.

FREEZE DRYING

This method is similar to dehydrating in that you are removing moisture from food to prolong their shelf-life. However, freeze drying involves freezing the plant matter before it is dried via sublimation. This means that ice is turned into vapor without turning into a liquid first. This leaves the final product with a very porous structure, i.e. it is crunchy.

Freeze drying requires a specific machine with a vacuum pump. Harvest Right is one company that produces reliable freeze dryers for the home market.

Freeze dried food lasts almost forever if stored in mylar bags with oxygen absorbers. However, we find that we love eating our freeze dried foods within a year. Try to get a little kid to stop munching on freeze dried strawberries or pineapple. And then try to stop momma from using her (freeze-dried) homemade garlic powder.

Because of the cost of something like this, you might want to pool a few

Split screen with freeze-dried garlic on the top and finished screen on the bottom

friends together and try a freeze dryer sharing program. Just remember that some consider it a loud machine. You will want to run it somewhere like a basement or garage.

PACKED IN OLIVE OIL

Cooked veggies packed in olive oil and vinegar will last for 3-4 months. The ratio of oil to vinegar is 2:1.
The cooked vegetables must be completely submerged. Any fresh or uncooked elements like garlic or dill can be added, but it will only hold for a week or so.

Once you have arranged your elements and covered them in the olive oil, vinegar, and salt mixture you can then freeze this to help it last longer.

OTHER OPTIONS

Jams and jellies, packing in honey, dehydrating and making food powders, baking into breads and freezing are all other options that you have for food preservation. Your number of options basically depends on your resources and level of ambition.

Also, take into account what you are actually going to like. Pickles are not for everyone. But then again, my son loves pickled okra, but not the pickled green tomatoes. Sometimes it's specific to the type of vegetable or the spice mix that you add.

Using watercolor jives with garden drawings

Nasturtium growing on a trellis inside greenhouse

08

Looking Back: Troubleshooting, Seed Saving, & Reminiscing

>> This book will help you start gardening with your kids, but, as with any journey, there are bound to be set-backs. Let's review some of the most common questions that new gardeners have and leave a little room to reminisce about the good times!

Troubleshooting: Q and A

•• This Q & A will not be exhaustive, but hopefully it will let you know that you are not alone. Any problem that you are facing has been faced and overcome before. If you don't find your answer here, feel free to check the Index to refer back and see if the answer is already somewhere in the book.

>> ### Some types of seeds didn't sprout! What happened?

If only one type of your seeds did not sprout, but your other varieties did, it is probably the seed. Check the expiry or germination test date to make sure they are not too old. Also, they might have been incorrectly stored. Heat will kill seeds. Lastly, some seeds require extra steps to germinate. Go online to see if they needed to be pre-soaked, scarred, or stratified.

None of my seeds sprouted! Ugh, what happened?

This is most likely a soil problem, but it can also be inconsistent watering. If you used soil from your property or from a local, untested source, it could be contaminated. To test this out, try a test sprouting with peas or tomatoes. They will be sensitive to any contaminants and will not grow in contaminated soil. Then try sprouting seeds in store-bought organic seed starting mix and see it they germinate.

My seedlings were doing awesome and then I planted them and they died. Help!?!

Once again, this can be a contaminated soil or compost problem. Do a test germination to see if you can get anything to sprout in that soil. Otherwise, it can be stress-induced. Heat, water, wind, and direct sunshine can stress a seedling to death. Make sure to acclimate your seedlings before moving them out, and plant them on a shady day if possible. Shade netting can also be used to help shield them while they get used to the garden.

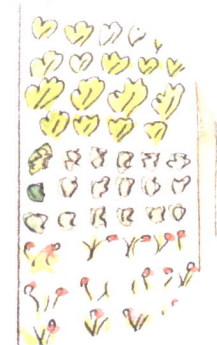

The best laid plans are just the start on a powerful learning journey

My vegetables were starting to develop their fruit (tomatoes, melons, peppers, whatever) and then the fruit rotted and fell off before it was ripe.

<<

Ooh. Been there. This one can be pests, inconsistent watering, or nutritional.

Stink bugs on tomatoes will cause young fruit to fall off. Inconsistent watering and a lack of calcium with melons will cause blossom end rot. Egg shells can be used to add calcium to the soil.

I am overwhelmed! Pests, weeds, my kids. You name it. What should I do?

Look, your mental health is number one. This whole gardening with kids thing is a learning experience. It's gaining wisdom. It's getting outside and having fun. I'm not saying stop the second something is not fun, but don't drag yourself over coals if aphids have won or a drought is wreaking havoc on your water supply. You can always stop or pause and come back to gardening later.

Here's a few ways to take a break.
1) Adjust your mindset. You are not giving up. You are prioritizing your happiness and, therefore, the happiness of your family.
2) Just tear it out. If you have one plant that you just can't deal with, like a curly kale that is covered in aphids and you can't seem to kill the little guys because they are all in the nooks and crannies, take it out and start over with something else.
3) Get help from your community. This works great for when you have an abundance of produce that you just don't have to time to harvest. This builds good will too over time. Maybe they can pull a few weeds while they are at it.

Quick pickled radishes are a great treat on tacos or in a salad

Seed Saving & Reminiscing

∨
∨

Reminiscing and digesting information go hand-in-hand. Speaking of digestion, make sure to add your tasting notes to your journals. This works especially well for canned or stored good so you can remember what they taste like so you can tell others.

Seed saving, dehydrating, and storing help to create a sense of closure to the growing year

At the end of the growing season, it's time to take a break and reflect. It's also time to save your seeds for next year.

Metaphorically, you already have seeds for a new journey next year, the seeds of knowledge, but you might need some practical tips for collecting vegetable and herb seeds from a variety of different types of plants.

SEED SAVING

First we need to talk about a couple of management issues. Cross-breeding and organic growing represent their own issues in regards to seed saving. If you grew more than one type of a particular plant, then the pollinators that visited your flowers might have cross-pollinated them. So your cherry tomatoes and your Cherokee purple tomatoes may have crossed and now the seeds that you collect from them will be a hybrid.

For some varieties and types like tomatoes, this seems pretty straightforward, but for other plants - things get weird. Zucchini and some species of winter squash can cross-pollinate because they are both members of the species Curcurbita pepo. The fruit that you get this year from both will look normal, but their seeds may produce a hybrid.

One year we had kabocha squash and delicata squash cross-pollinate and the result was a beautifully striped orange kabochacata or delibocha. Probably because both species

have edible skin and a creamy texture when cooked, this cross worked out. By the way, they were not supposed to be able to cross, but they seemed to, or maybe the zucchini pollen got in their too and worked some pollination magic.

Here is a list of the squashes that will definitely cross because they are in the same family.

C. pepo: Pattypan, Acorn squash, Straightneck, Zucchini, Gourds, Delicata

C. moschata: Butternut squash, Crookneck, Long Island Cheese Pumpkin, Tromboncino

C. maxima: Hubbard, Buttercup, Arikara, Candy Roaster, Kabocha

For things like tomatoes and peppers, you can save the seeds from ripe fruit. Tomato seeds have a little jelly around them. You can float them in water and the jelly will disperse (technically ferment) after a day or so.

For things like zucchini, let one get really big and save those seeds. For okra, let the okra pod get brown on the plant and split, and then they are ready.

Peas and beans should also be left on the vine until the pods turn brown and crispy. It's a good idea to mark which ones you want to save with a ribbon or tag so your little munchers don't attack them. Mark off the ones that look the best, the biggest, and the brightest color for future seed saving.

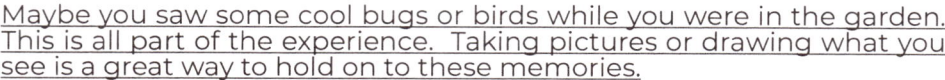

Maybe you saw some cool bugs or birds while you were in the garden. This is all part of the experience. Taking pictures or drawing what you see is a great way to hold on to these memories.

Saving the seeds of cilantro and wisdom

Salad greens will bolt, as will basil and cilantro. You can save those tiny seeds by collecting the entire pod and then scraping it over a fine mesh to separate the seed from the chaff.

Sunflowers, those majestic giants of the garden, are pretty straightforward. You just want to make sure that you get to them before the birds do. It is one of our favorite yearly activities to separate out the individual seeds from the fractal pattern on the flower head.

This is also a good time to remember that if you did grow a non-organic or GMO variety of plant in your garden, then these traits will be passed down and could compromise your other crops if they cross-breed.

REMINISCING

Let's take a little stroll down memory lane, starting with your goals. You remember those, from the beginning of the book? Did you laugh, love, and grow? I hope so. Did your kids learn something? I know they did.

If you have been keeping up with your journal and your kids have been keeping up with theirs, you will have a yearbook of plants. On the next page, we have a sample of what it might look like if you grew and recorded Sugar Snap Peas.

You can go over your favorites

"Remember when" is a great prompt to jog some memories.

together and your least liked and why. You may find that the most challenging plant was the most tasty. There are so many lessons to learn from nature.

If you don't know it already, I learned a few things from nature and gardening with kids that I want to share with you. You can do this and your kid's can do this. You will grow closer together, bond over plants, and laugh over silly garden stuff because gardening is fun. When my son runs around sneaking bites of sorrel, lemon balm, and picking all the ripe tomatoes and eating them. I joke with him, "Hey, buddy! Whatcha doing'? You sneaky, sneak. Don't eat all the good ones. Save some for me." Do you think I mind that he is eating vegetables and "sneaking around the garden"? Nope, not one bit.

Gardening is a life skill and one that you will strengthen over time, like a muscle. You just have to use it. Use each year with your littles as a way to expand on the previous year's knowledge. Help your kids to become experts in the field and they will have a life-long love of all things gardening and growing.

I hope that this book has given you some confidence and enough knowledge to garden with your kids using organic permaculture principles. I hope they "steal" all the good veggies and eat them up every day you are in the garden.

Plant Name:

Sugar Snap Pea

(Pisum sativum)

> **Seed started date:** 3/1/22
> **Seeding planted date:** 3/22/22

Identifying Characteristics (aka What it looks like): Long vine w/ opposing leaves. Spirally tendrils that grab.

Secondary Characteristics (flowers, growth habit): Flowers are small and white, grows faster than the snow peas, tendrils really help it climb

Any pests? Nope.

Beneficial insects? Bees! Some hoverflies, too.

Easy to harvest or do you need a tool? Easy, pop off w/ fingernail

Problems, brown leaves, or mildew: Only lasted until the summer got hot

Taste? So sweet. Yum, yum.

Seed Collecting Notes: We tied a ribbon to some plant to make sure we did not pick them. Let them mature & dry on vine.

Do you want to grow this again? Definitely! 2 times.

Favorite thing about this plant: Fun garden snack!!

Kid's Garden Journal

Plant Name: Sugar Snap Pea

DLING

MATURE PLANT

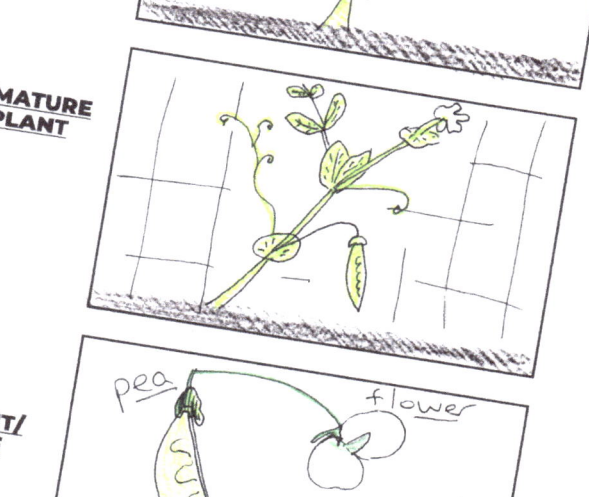

FRUIT/ LEAF

pea   flower

tendril

Index

Thank You For Your Support

Thanks to Nick and Xavier for supporting me during this endeavor and thank you to the Oregon Permaculture Design Course teachers for helping me to be a life-long learner.

Thank you to my proofreaders, Cara, Angela, Teresa, and Lindsey!

Like us on Instagram
@LandArkTN
@HerbArkTN

Christine Rosakranse is a Stanford-trained PhD, mother, farmer, educator, and author. Not necessarily in that order. Her previous scientific studies on compassion and social media turned her into a farmer and aspiring luddite shortly after graduation. After learning about Permaculture Design and organic methods from Oregon State University, she decided to teach those principles to her own son and as many families as she could reach. She wants you to be organic, happy and healthy!

LandArkTN.com/
@LandArkTN
@HerbArkTN